MW00830005

—— 40 ——

# Breakthrough Declarations

POWERFUL PRAYERS TO
HEAL PAST HURTS, MAKE FUTURE PROVISION,
AND INVITE JESUS INTO YOUR TIMELINE

## TROY A. BREWER

DESTINY IMAGE® PUBLISHERS, INC.

P.O. Box 310, Shippensburg, PA 17257-0310

*"Promoting Inspired Lives."*

This book and all other Destiny Image and Destiny Image Fiction books are available at Christian bookstores and distributors worldwide.

Cover design by Eileen Rockwell

Interior design by Terry Clifton

For more information on foreign distributors, call 717-532-3040.

Reach us on the Internet: www.destinyimage.com.

ISBN 13 TP: 978-0-7684-6110-7

ISBN 13 eBook: 978-0-7684-6109-1

ISBN 13 HC: 978-0-7684-6108-4

For Worldwide Distribution, Printed in the U.S.A.

1 2 3 4 5 6 7 8 / 25 24 23 22 21

# Contents

# Welcome and Introduction

Hello, my friend!

We all know a house built on sand won't last. Right on! Foundations matter. If the foundation is off, anything built on top of it will be faulty. Using Jesus Christ as our Chief Cornerstone, you and I will dive into this foundational teaching on time, redemption, and the transformational practice I like to call *Redeeming Your Timeline*.

To do that, we'll use five basic premises. A premise is a big deal in the Bible. You can find them easily if you know to look for the "if/then" or "therefore" statements in scripture.

> *Therefore if the Son makes you free, you shall be free indeed* (John 8:36).
>
> *He who is of God hears God's words; therefore you do not hear, because you are not of God* (John 8:47).

A premise follows a line of logic: if *this* is true, then/therefore, so is *that*. As I noted in my book *Redeeming Your Timeline*, it's like when Jesus says, "Now that you understand this idea, from there we move forward." The Bible is loaded with a titanic 1,220

1

"therefores"—76 in the book of John alone. Here in America, 76 is a number synonymous with freedom—and you all know what a "freedom fanatic" I am! This revelation of redeeming time will set you free from the guilt and shame of your past.

## Setting the Stage of Time

I do not know when time began, but I think I know when time began for Adam. Adam may have lived for billions of years or 24 hours before he disobeyed God and got kicked off the glorious reservation called Eden. We don't know because, outside of the seven days of creation, there is no clear reference to time. That is, until sin shows up.

You may say, "But Pastor Troy, the Bible clearly says the evening and the morning in each day of creation marked a day so we are talking about a true 24-hour period."

Know this: I have no trouble calling the seven days of creation seven "days" because that's what the Bible calls it. I am not smarter than the Bible, so there is no need for me to fix it. I also do not mind pointing out that the sun was not created until the fourth day. That means the first three days had nothing to do with the consecutive period of time during which the sun is above the horizon—what you and I call a day.

There is also this argument about time:

*But, beloved, do not forget this one thing, that with the Lord one day is as a thousand years, and a thousand years as one day* (2 Peter 3:8).

*For a thousand years in Your sight are like yesterday when it is past, and like a watch in the night* (Psalm 90:4).

Again, I don't know when time began, but I believe the "day" Adam sinned turned into a very real 24-hour day as we know it now. He fell from what Sir Isaac Newton understood as "absolute time" (I call this "redeemed" time) into what Einstein describes as "relative" time (what I call "unredeemed" time). You are a gifted learner, so you can get this.

## The Trapdoor of Time

The clock began ticking for Adam when he ate the fruit of the Knowledge of Good and Evil. Having lost access to the Tree of Life for his own protection, the laws of entropy—a.k.a. the Second Law of Thermodynamics—began to apply to him. He began to age and deteriorate. He was now dealing with the reality of unredeemed time where sin and death reign.

*For the wages of sin is death, but the gift of God is eternal life in Christ Jesus our Lord* (Romans 6:23).

Sin and death are in perfect continuum. If you get rid of one, you get rid of the other. The moment Adam was contaminated with sin, he was owned by death. Death reigns in time, space, and matter.

Can you imagine? Adam walked with God uninhibited by the space between two distances. He wasn't ruled by the laws of gravity or physical limitations. He was more super than natural. He had dominion over time, space, and matter just like Jesus after the resurrection. He could walk through a closed door or cover large distances in the blink of an eye. Then, in one horrible moment, Adam's experience changed into something different.

> *Then the eyes of both of them were opened, and they knew that they were naked; and they sewed fig leaves together and made themselves coverings* (Genesis 3:7).

His worldview changed and immediately he and his beautiful wife are trying to stitch their broken lives back together. They are now about the business of covering up shameful things.

This brutal new environment meant things that shouldn't happen, happen often. Adam was introduced to anxiety, fear, and shame. Now subject to the elements (matter), his body would have to fight off cancer and disease. He would have to find shelter. He saw his first thorn and felt his first bead of sweat. It was a different kind of bad. Nothing about dreaming here; everything about surviving for as long as you can before death finally catches you on another bad day. This was worse than being Davey Crockett at the Alamo!

Death. The fear of it paralyzes folks and keeps them from really living. Do you feel like death is stalking you? I'll let you in on a little secret that will halt the horror: Death is not stalking you. It already has you. Adam was fallen in every way a person could be fallen and he took each and every person born into this human experience with him. We are born already dying.

This, my friend, is why it's important to understand the reality of redeeming time. God hates death. It's one of the reasons Jesus wept for Lazarus despite knowing he would be resurrected. Death was not God's plan for us, but that didn't stop Him from finding a way to fix the problem. God has always deeply loved you, so He had a plan to trump the serpent's plan.

> *So the Lord God said to the serpent: "Because you have done this, you are cursed more than all cattle, and more than every beast of the field; on your belly you shall go, and you shall eat dust all the days of your life. And I will put enmity between you and the woman, and between your seed and her Seed; he shall bruise your head, and you shall bruise His heel"* (Genesis 3:14-15).

At the very beginning of time, on the day Adam sinned, God gives His very first promise concerning redemption by hinting at the birth of a Messiah Redeemer. That Redeemer—Jesus— would walk the earth 4,000 years after Adam and He would turn back the clock for all who believe in Him through the gift of redemption.

Redemption is a really big deal. It means that something dead can be alive again, and redemption is absolutely tied to time. Time was the ace up God's holy sleeve to insure an environment where a redemptive work could take place. That's why I call time "a gift from God," and you should consider it a gift as well. Just remember that God is good, all the time. Everything He has for you is good.

In the scriptures, devotions, and declarations you are about to read, you'll unwrap that gift and learn how to use it in your life and the lives of those around you. If you need a breakthrough, a fresh start, or a new perspective, you will find it in these pages, I promise you that.

Remember that you are a bad motor scooter. God is always going to be with you so you can always receive the best He has for you! So, enjoy the journey of redeeming your timeline. You'll find supernatural skillsets for healing past wounds, calming future anxieties, and discovering rest in the now on every page.

*Troy*

# Understanding Time and Eternity

Do you understand the makeup of the created thing called "time"? Most people don't, though it's a common part of our everyday experience and expressive language.

We say things like, "Time is critical," "It's about time," "Time is money," and "In the nick of time." Time flies, marches on, and somehow gets onto our hands. Yes, we talk about time all the time, but do we have a true working knowledge of what these seconds, minutes, hours, and days really mean? The honest answer for most of us is, "No."

Let me tell you, my friend, the reason we can measure, number, and predict time is because we as mortal humans are shackled by it—literal prisoners from our first to our last breath. When brother Adam and his sidekick Eve (pun intended) bit into the serpent's lie that God is not really good, a trapdoor opened beneath them and they fell into a timeline.

Know this: While we are subject to time, God doesn't live in that realm.

**Premise 1: God created time and is not subject to or shackled by it in any way.**

God has a plan that He wants you to understand. If I can understand it, I know you can too! In the following pages, we will put time under a microscope. We'll find out what it is, what it's not, and how time compares to eternity. It's a big subject, so let's dive right in!

*Troy*

# Day 1

## What Is Time?

*To everything there is a season, and a time for every purpose under heaven* (Ecclesiastes 3:1).

Oh, we are all about time! But do we really know what time even is? I've had a lot of years to think about it and I have to tell you, my worldview on the subject is this: Time is a gift from God. God *gave* you time.

Time is something that can be measured, numbered, and predicted by common people. Because of this, time is an environment created for our safety and sanity. Think of it like this: When you are expecting a baby, what is the first thing you do? Set up the nursery.

Just think about it this way: The nursery is a safe place for the baby to explore the world within confines that will cause it to develop in a positive manner. That is what time does for us. It gives us boundaries in which we can understand all that's around us without blowing our minds.

My friend, we need to understand time in order to partner with God's purpose for us because time is the place where purpose is accomplished and transformation takes place. Time is not to be feared. It is to be managed well and that's what this book is all about—understanding the gift of time so it can be used in a way that glorifies the Maker of all space and time while moving you and me forward in our purpose and destiny.

Without time, there would be no such thing as destiny—an expected end. And man, I want not only a good end to my life but an excellent end to my life, just like you do.

> *For I know the thoughts that I think toward you, saith the Lord, thoughts of peace, and not of evil, to give you an expected end* (Jeremiah 29:11 KJV).

Do you see it? Time is God's gift of purpose and destiny—a reason to be and a forever destination in His presence. Today is the day the Lord has made. Let us, you and I, rejoice and be glad for the gift of today (see Ps. 118:24).

## I Declare in Jesus' Name...

- Time is a gift from God. I am thankful He has trusted me with it.
- The Lord has a great big purpose for me. I will partner with Him to go after it today.
- The thoughts the Lord has for me are for my good and never my harm. I trust Him with my life—my entire life.

10

- I will steward this season of my life well. I will manage my time and let Jesus transform me into His image.
- I declare I have an expected end in the Kingdom of God. He will accomplish His destiny for me!

*Day 2*

# The Dawn of Time

*In the beginning God created the heaven and the earth* (Genesis 1:1).

I love studying first and last things including first and last sentences. It's been said the first sentence of a book is "make or break." It's the thing that piques the imagination and draws the reader in. Dickens knew it when he penned, "It was the best of times. It was the worst of times," as the opening line of his masterpiece *A Tale of Two Cities.*

Just like that, *The Hitchhiker's Guide to the Galaxy* opens with this whopper: "Far out in the uncharted backwaters of the unfashionable end of the western spiral arm of the Galaxy lies a small, unregarded yellow sun."

As infamous as these opening lines may be, nothing tops the mind-grabbing, heart-pounding words of God Almighty penned by brother Moses himself on an animal skin scroll in the wilderness of Sinai. With these words, spirit and science meet creation and continuum:

*In the beginning*—that's time.

*God created the heavens*—now we're introduced to space.

*And the earth*—matter enters the scene.

Time, space, and matter in the first sentence of an ancient book that chronicles an eternal God, His creation, and His crazy cool love for that creation. In one sentence, the Lord spells out what took mankind and Minkowski 5,668 years to discover—the space-time continuum. *Continuum* is the genius way of saying, "If this thing exists, so does this other thing because you can't have one without the other."

These three elements are inexplicably intertwined throughout nature. You can't have space without time to get from one place to another, and you need matter to fill space. It all works together and it paints a picture of the One who created it all.

Before the end of the first chapter, the Triune God is introduced and the true continuum is revealed:

> *Then God said, "Let **Us** make man in **Our** image, according to **Our** likeness; let them have dominion over the fish of the sea, over the birds of the air, and over the cattle, over all the earth and over every creeping thing that creeps on the earth." So God created man in **His** own image; in the image of God **He** created him; male and female **He** created them* (Genesis 1:26-27).

Not One, but three. Inseparable yet distinctly individual. Time, space, and matter are the tangible representation of the Father, the Son (Word), and the Holy Spirit—the original continuum. Each has its own unique qualities, personality, and purpose, yet together there is a supernatural synergy that transcends space and time.

The One who started it all gave us a crystal clear picture of Himself in everything we see and experience. Once you see Him in that mind-bending sentence, you can't un-see Him. Do you? Do you see Him in this thing called time? He's there. Trust me. God has only good and wonderful things in store for you. So declare these things, my friend, and believe them!

## I Declare in Jesus' Name...

- Time is God's special creation. His nature and His will are seen in it and through it.
- Time will someday pass away, but the power of the Triune God will never pass away.
- God wants me to know and understand Him. I will chase after Him in the pages of scripture today and every day.
- Time, space, and matter were created by God. They belong to Him and He uses them for His purposes.
- God created time as a gift to me. He will accomplish His purpose for me through time.

# Outside of Time

*And God said unto Moses, I Am That I Am: and he said, Thus shalt thou say unto the children of Israel, I Am hath sent me unto you. And God said moreover unto Moses, Thus shalt thou say unto the children of Israel, the Lord God of your fathers, the God of Abraham, the God of Isaac, and the God of Jacob, hath sent me unto you: this is my name for ever, and this is my memorial unto all generations* (Exodus 3:14-15 KJV).

Did you know the Almighty God of the Universe has a calling card? He does. Let me explain.

Unlike you and me, God does not have a past, present, or future. He made that crystal clear when He appeared to Moses in the form of a burning bush and said the immortal (pun intended) words, "I Am That I Am."

No apologies, no excuses, or explanations. God drops the bombshell, "I just Am." Nobody created Him. He was never formed or fashioned. He had no beginning and He has no end. He just is and He has always been. No birthdays or anniversaries. No father or mother. God simply *is*.

Eternity. A place outside of time without a ticking clock. This is where the Great I Am lives. Forever is hard to fathom for us whose lives are measured by time, ruled by distance, and dependent on matter. God is subject to none of these things. They are subject to Him. Time does not define God. He defines it and us.

So when God name-drops, Moses' jaw drops, and so, my friends, should yours. With the simple words "I Am That I Am," God gives us His eternal credentials and they are impressive!

> *This is My name forever, and this is My memorial to all generations* (Exodus 3:15).

God is saying, "No matter what happens with you, Moses, no matter what happens on this rock I placed third in line from the sun on the outer edge of one of a million galaxies, My presence and personhood stand firm—immovable. I have always been and always will be—and all of My creation in and throughout this tiny place called time will know it."

"I Am That I Am" is more than an introduction. It is state of being without boundaries or limitations. It is the literal picture of eternity—God's home and, someday soon, yours and mine as well. It is ridonkulous the wonderful plans He has for you and me!

## I Declare in Jesus' Name...

- I love the name of the Lord. He is the Great I Am and has a place for me in eternity.
- I will tell my generations the name of the Lord. He will be our refuge in times of plenty and in want.
- Time is God's creation to protect me and nurture me. I will use my time to glorify Him.
- I will pursue the purposes God has for me this day. I am His and He is mine forever.
- Eternity is my home and the Great I Am is my God. I want to be where He is.

# Heaven's View of Time

*So the Lord said to Moses, "I will also do this thing that you have spoken; for you have found grace in My sight, and I know you by name."*

*And he said, "Please, show me Your glory."*

*Then He said, "I will make all My goodness pass before you, and I will proclaim the name of the Lord before you. I will be gracious to whom I will be gracious, and I will have compassion on whom I will have compassion." But He said, "You cannot see My face; for no man shall see Me, and live." And the Lord said, "Here is a place by Me, and you shall stand on the rock. So it shall be, while My glory passes by, that I will put you in the cleft of the rock, and will cover you with My hand while I pass by. Then I will take away My hand, and you shall see My back; but My face shall not be seen"* (Exodus 33:17-23).

In this amazing account of favor and friendship, the Bible introduces heaven's view of time. So, let's go back in time.

At age 40, Moses, the Jew who didn't belong in the house of the Egyptians and wasn't welcome in the camp of his own people, had run away and lived with another group he didn't belong to—the Midianites. After forty years with them, he finally found somebody he belonged to—God.

Following a supernatural showdown with Pharaoh, the most powerful man on the planet, Moses learned who the real Deliverer was, and it wasn't him. For his faithfulness, God granted this man, His friend, a once-in-a-millennia request and Moses went for it, saying, "Show me your glory." He wanted to see the visible awesomeness of God.

The relationship Moses had with God was special. So was the revelation God had for him. Upon request, God replied that His awesomeness would not be seen head-on. Still, He had a plan and we find it when Moses went to the top of the mountain and saw the backside of God.

In a tiny glimpse of God's glory through the lens of redemption, Moses saw the goodness of God from that moment backward in time past. Every good thing God had done and every good way God had been in the past, I believe Moses saw it all in a game-changing glimpse of God's backside.

You might not know it, but this is a reference to a timeline. Everything under the law deals with present/past tense, so this is the way God revealed His glory, or visible awesomeness, to

Moses—in present/past tense. From that moment backward. So, when Moses put his ancient feather to the animal skin canvas, these were the epic words he would introduce to the world as the written Word of God:

> *In the beginning God created the heavens and the earth* (Genesis 1:1).

It is our awesome introduction to an indivisible God. Written by an ancient, barefoot man in the Middle East, these words are a reference to God creating time, space, and matter all at once. Amazing, isn't it? A Spirit God with three identities producing three dimensions—boundaries for the safety and well-being of His creation. When you grasp this revelation, like Moses, you will be forever changed.

## I Declare in Jesus' Name...

- I want to see the glory of the Lord. I know He is good yesterday, today, and forever.
- I am God's friend. Like Moses before me, I run into the tent of meeting to be in His presence.
- God has been good in my past and my present. I know I can trust Him with my future.
- Like Moses, I belong to God. He is my home and my refuge.
- I embrace the plan God has for me. I welcome transformation today and every day.

*Day 5*

# From Everlasting

*The Eternity of God, and Man's Frailty (A Prayer of Moses the man of God)*
*Lord, You have been our dwelling place in all generations. Before the mountains were brought forth, or ever You had formed the earth and the world, even from everlasting to everlasting, You are God* (Psalm 90:1-2).

The Psalms call the place God dwells "everlasting." A place where there is no time. No space. No matter. A destination outside the bounds of time where real life exists because the Giver of all life is ever present there. Make no mistake. God does not live in time. We do. But someday, if we tap into His everlasting goodness, we will be invited into eternity.

That's why the Bible says in Psalm 42:7 that *"Deep calls unto deep."* God takes us from "good" into the extraordinary and gives us a glimpse of a place without time.

*From everlasting to everlasting* (Psalm 41:13).

You have an everlasting within you and it's called your spirit. It's this everlasting part of you that calls to the Everlasting that is Him. The Lord revealed this to King Solomon. When that brother asked the Lord for wisdom, he got supernatural insight into the very heart of God.

> *He has made everything beautiful in its time. Also He has put eternity in their hearts* (Ecclesiastes 3:11).

A piece of eternity—God's dwelling place—has been lovingly placed inside you. Some call it a "God-shaped hole" in your heart. However you picture it, make no mistake—it's your homing beacon. Throughout your life it is activated by God's Spirit and it calls to you. Do you have ears to hear? Most do not.

They mistake the voice of God for the love of man. They try to fill that eternal space with money, fame, power, position, addiction—the list goes on. None of these things satisfy. None of them *fit*. The things of the world can never take the place of an eternal God in your heart or your place in His. Hear the voice of God crying out to you from the many waters. Cry out to Him today. Let the deep in you call out to the deep in Him. Let His eternal peace rule in your heart and be filled by the everlasting, satisfying Jesus.

## I Declare in Jesus' Name...

- I have ears to hear the deep in Jesus calling out to the deep in me. I will answer and let the everlasting God take His place in my heart.
- I renounce the things of this world that have taken the Lord's rightful place in my life. Nothing of the world satisfies. Only Jesus can make me whole.
- I claim my place in God's family. I have a place at His table in His home called Eternity.
- Time is God's gift to me. I am thankful for His lovingkindness.

*Day 6*

# The Original Big Bang

*Love is patient, love is kind. It does not envy, it does not boast, it is not proud. It does not dishonor others, it is not self-seeking, it is not easily angered, it keeps no record of wrongs. Love does not delight in evil but rejoices with the truth. It always protects, always trusts, always hopes, always perseveres. Love never fails* (1 Corinthians 13:4-8 NIV).

One night in Austin, Texas, I was playing guitar in a Christian rock band called Destiny. We were at a place called The Liberty Lunch. In the middle of praying for a young married couple sitting at the bar, I looked up and saw a framed statement among pictures of crop duster airplanes, guitar players, and Texas folk art. It was a quote that changed my life:

"Time is God's way of keeping everything from happening at once."

*Boom!* It shook me like a thunderbolt. My very foundation began to wonder, to question, and consider the implications of such a statement. I prayed out loud and asked God, "Sir, why wouldn't You want everything to happen at one time?"

That night, God began to talk to me about time.

It turns out, time is a tool God uses for our benefit. Because He is good, He wants us to move from past to future, darkness to light, and from death to life. He likes progression and forward movement. If He is going to move us from history to destiny, time is the only place something like that can happen.

Unlike eternity where everything is and always will be, time is a created space for humanity. It is the only place where God can look at us and say, "That was then but this is now." Without time, we would have no past—only a present. Any mistakes we made, we would own forever. Forever is a mighty long time to be saddled with guilt and shame. It's a good thing our God *is* Love (see 1 John 4:8).

Love could not stand to see you riddled with guilt and stained by shame. Those things aren't even allowed in the presence of God. My friend, guilt and shame are the result of sin, and sin— anything that breaks God's heart—is not allowed in eternity with God. The only way for you and I, who are guilty of sin, to spend eternity with God in heaven is through the gift of time.

In time, there is a past that can be overcome. It can be forgiven, redeemed, and restored. That is why Love keeps no record of wrongs. It protects. It perseveres, and it never, never fails.

# I Declare in Jesus' Name...

- I serve a God of Love. He does not keep a record of my wrongs.
- Time is God's gift to rid me of sin, guilt and shame. I am no longer a slave to sin and darkness because God has forgiven me.
- I do not fear the future. My God has made a way for me.
- I am not bound by my past. My God has a plan for my life.

*Day 7*

# Time Is a Matter of Perspective

*Then God said, "Let there be lights in the firmament*
*of the heavens to divide the day from the night; and*
*let them be for signs and seasons, and for days and*
*years; and let them be for lights in the firmament of*
*the heavens to give light on the earth"; and it was so*
(Genesis 1:14-15).

The word firmament is a fancy word that means "from a certain perspective." Just like the heavens were created to be viewed and understood from our perspective on earth, God didn't create time from His point of view, rather from our own.

Remember, even science tells us that time is relative to the observer. I learned an important principle several years back sitting in my truck waiting for a train to pass. A seemingly never-ending lineup of 100-plus, graffiti-covered box cars had me almost hypnotized when a God thought hit me.

At about train car number 40, I looked down the track and couldn't tell how long the train was. I wished I had a helicopter to get an aerial view of the entire length of the train. In my 10-pound head, I began to visualize what the train looked like from way above.

Then it hit me: From my perspective, I can see only one moment at a time—like my perspective of each passing train car. It goes by slowly and is only a tiny fragment of the entire train. However, from God's perspective, 1,000 feet up, He can see the beginning, the middle, and the end of my timeline all at the same time.

My friend, our view of time is so myopic, or nearsighted, we can only perceive the moment, or the part of the train we are walking in right now. But God's view of time is not limited because He is not subject to time at all. He's not just on the train. He is actually above it all. He can see the beginning and the end, right now.

What does that mean? God is not subject to time. He can go into car number one or car 100 at will, which means He can go into your future or 20 years into your past without breaking a sweat. That's how I know Jesus is a time traveler and your past is no problem for the Prince of Peace. He made all the galaxies, so that's no problem for Him at all!

## I Declare in Jesus' Name...

- Nothing is too hard for You, Jesus. You created time and you can go in and out of it wherever and whenever you want.

- I have a new perspective on time. Time is subject to You. You can travel anywhere in my timeline and do so for my good.
- You have given me eyes to see and ears to hear your prophetic word. I declare dreams, visions, and the gift of supernatural insight are mine.
- I am not chained by my past. You have made me free so I am also free of past hurts, habits, and hangups.

*Day 8*

# Today Is the Day

*Those who first heard the good news of deliverance failed to enter into that realm of faith's rest because of their unbelieving hearts. Yet the fact remains that we still have the opportunity to enter into the faith-rest life and experience the fulfillment of the promise! For God still has ordained a day for us to enter into called "Today." For it was long afterwards that God repeated it in David's words, "If only today you would listen to his voice and do not harden your hearts!"* (Hebrews 4:6-7 TPT)

Did you know the Lord has a day set aside for you to get yourself saved and enter into this eternal family? He sure does. So, when is the most auspicious of days? Today.

Whoever first penned the words "There's no time like the present" was a genius. Either that, or that brother knew God on a way next-level basis.

It's true. There is no time like the present, right now, this moment. It's the only time you'll experience the things you are right this moment under the circumstances you are experiencing them. Just like that, there is a set of circumstances around the date and time that you take Jesus up on His generous offer to be with Him in Paradise. He's got a terrific place planned for you!

> *For He says: "In an acceptable time I have heard you,*
> *and in the day of salvation I have helped you." Behold,*
> *now is the accepted time; behold, now is the day of sal-*
> *vation* (2 Corinthians 6:2).

My friend, none of us are guaranteed tomorrow so today is all we have. Today is the best time to do a lot of things like:

Forgive those people who hurt you.

Tell someone you're sorry and ask their forgiveness.

Put that grudge behind you.

Thank that person for their kindness.

Call that person you've been meaning to call but never do.

Say that secret thing hidden on your heart out loud and see what God does with it.

Today is also the best time to humble your heart and ask God to forgive you, free you, and give you the eternal life He offers. My friend, you can trust Him! I have, and what a difference it's made. He sure won't disappoint you! Today is your day to enter into that eternal rest or peace.

If you've already done that, then I praise God with you!

*The Lord shall preserve your going out and your coming in from this time forth, and even forevermore* (Psalm 121:8).

## I Declare in Jesus' Name...

- Today is the day of my salvation. I say "YES" to the gift of eternal life in heaven with Jesus.

- I am Yours, Jesus, and You are mine. I belong to You fully and will follow You.

- I am grateful to be part of the family of God. I am no longer an orphan but a son of the Most High God.

- Holy Spirit, You are welcome here. Make my heart Your home and fill me with Your presence and power.

- I am a new creation. Old things have passed away and I am transformed by the power of God. I have a hope and a future in His Kingdom.

# A Prayer for Understanding Time

*Father God, You created time and it's literally in Your hands. Make my times and my seasons exalt Your holy name. Let Your goodness pass before me as I see my days. Cause me to be in perfect alignment with every Kingdom purpose in every time and season You are trusting me with.*

*Though I know Your blood has blotted out my sins forever, I know there is damage and decay that still affects my life today. I ask You, Jesus, to travel throughout my past. Bring to mind any place that needs redemption. Bring to mind hurts that are buried but not forgiven, relationships that were broken and never mended, and curses that were put in motion that need to be broken. I want to redeem these things so my heart and mind can be whole.*

*Lord, I know You don't mind my humanity because You made me human. I also know You're the only One who can straighten out my messes. So, I depend on You to do that for me.*

*I thank You, Holy Spirit, for the work You are doing in my heart. I make my heart Your home. I give You exclusive rights to uproot any residue from the past I have not dealt with, especially times I have hurt others, so it can be redeemed. I give you control of my life and my times. Amen.*

*I love You, oh God of my past, present, and future. In Jesus' name, amen.*

*My times are in Your hand* (Psalm 31:15).

# Time Was Created for Great Works of Redemption!

As we discovered in last week's devotions, time is a big deal. We count it, waste it, pass it, and even kill it. As big of a deal as time is to the human experience, redemption is even bigger.

Redemption is a line in the sand that says, "That was then, but this is now." You are a new creation because you've put that line behind you. If there is no redemption, time is nothing but a slow death to all creation. If you make a big deal out of time, you have to make a big deal out of redemption—and we are going to do that in a really big way in the following pages.

My friend, know this about God's ingenious invention of time:

***Premise 2: God created time for the purpose of works of redemption.***

Why? Because He loves you too much to leave you in something that is limiting you. My friend, God always wants the very best for you.

*Troy*

# Worth the Wait!

*Where could I go from your Spirit? Where could I run and hide from your face? If I go up to heaven, you're there! If I go down to the realm of the dead, you're there too! If I fly with wings into the shining dawn, you're there! If I fly into the radiant sunset, you're there waiting!* (Psalm 139:7-9 TPT)

When it comes to the subject of redeeming your timeline, there is no verse that spells it out like Psalm 139. It literally shouts, "Jesus is a time traveler and His favorite destination is your past!"

Let's read it again, this time with some notes from me:

*Where could I go from your Spirit? Where could I run and hide from your face? If I go up to heaven [eternity], you're there! If I go down to the realm of the dead [also eternity], you're there too! If I fly with wings into the shining dawn [the future], you're there! If I fly into the radiant sunset [the past], you're there waiting!* (Psalm 139:7-9 TPT)

Why is Jesus waiting in your past? To redeem it! Jesus is such a redemption freak that He sacrificed His life to literally become sin for you to be counted sinless. See, if you have any kind of sin attached to you, you cannot be in the presence of God in His holy habitation of heaven.

"But Pastor Troy, the Bible says all our sins are forgiven—past, present, and future. If God doesn't keep a record of wrongs, why do I need Jesus to go into my past and redeem it?"

I'm so glad you asked! While it is so very true that God keeps no record of our wrongs, it's also very true that we do. We know we're forgiven, but we're haunted by past failures and mistakes. We're hunted by broken relationships and shattered hearts. Many of us can't forgive our past behavior or the things others have done to us. Our words and actions dog us because we can't let go.

Why is this such a big deal? Because it cripples your walk with the Lord and your testimony of Jesus to those around you. Living in the past will kill your promise and limit your future. It enslaves you and brings generational curses on your family. You cannot live the abundant life Jesus died to give you if you dwell on past hurts, habits, and hangups.

My friend, Jesus is so happy to travel to your past with the gift of redemption. Has it already been given to you? Yes. But if you need to revisit that place and mark it with His blood to give you the breakthrough you need, He's there. Waiting just for you.

# I Declare in Jesus' Name...

- I accept the gift of redemption Jesus died to give me—past, present, and future.

- I repent of beating myself up over my past. I will look to my future with confidence in Your plan, Lord.

- My future belongs to You, Lord God. I trust You with my purpose and destiny.

- I give my past to You today. I will no longer be defined by past failures and mistakes.

- Just as You keep no record of my wrongs, Lord, I declare the list I've been keeping to be null and void. You have paid the price and it is enough!

# And the Books Were Opened

*Lord, you know everything there is to know about me. You perceive every movement of my heart and soul, and you understand my every thought before it even enters my mind. You are so intimately aware of me, Lord. You read my heart like an open book and you know all the words I'm about to speak before I even start a sentence! You know every step I will take before my journey even begins. You've gone into my future to prepare the way, and in kindness you follow behind me to spare me from the harm of my past. You have laid your hand on me!* (Psalm 139:1-5 TPT)

Like I said yesterday, Psalm 139 in *The Passion Translation* is one of my very favorite passages that spells out God's principle of redeeming your timeline. To me, it screams, "Time was created especially for redemption!"

Read the above verses again. How can God know your movements before you make them and thoughts before you think them? How is it possible for Him to know all the words you'll speak before you start a sentence or your path before you take a step? Simple.

> *Declaring the end from the beginning, and from ancient times things that are not yet done, saying, "My counsel shall stand, and I will do all My pleasure"* (Isaiah 46:10).

Why does God declare the end from the beginning? Because the end—your final destination—is the most important thing to Him. He's already seen the *end* of your story and He's "working all things for your good" (see Rom. 8:28) through the pages of your life—today and yesterday. Yes, the Lord, like many of us, likes to read the end of the story before the beginning, and you are His favorite subject.

> *You are our epistle written in our hearts, known and read by all men; clearly you are an epistle of Christ, ministered by us, written not with ink but by the Spirit of the living God, not on tablets of stone but on tablets of flesh, that is, of the heart* (2 Corinthians 3:2-3).

In God's economy, your life is a literal book and time is something God actually reads. It's His record of your life—a transcript. Because He knows the end (the future) from the beginning (the past), He can go into your future to prepare the way and He has the capability to follow behind to spare you from the failures and fallout of the days before you met Him. Remember, your past is His favorite destination because Jesus wants to redeem those places so you can reach your "expected end" (see Jer. 29:11).

And the Word says He does this all in kindness with His hand upon you to guide you, hold you, stop you, and move you forward. Why? Because He knows your destination and it is good! In heaven, the books of our hearts will be opened before the Lord. Make sure your story is an awesome adventure filled with victory, redemption, and transformation—a mighty testimony of Jesus for the ages! He is the author and the finisher of your faith (see Heb. 12:2).

## I Declare in Jesus' Name...

- The Lord knows my end from the beginning. I will not fear the future or be defeated by my past.
- Jesus has redeemed me in every way. The pain of my past has been fully paid for by His blood. I will no longer dwell on it.
- I forgive those who hurt me or treated me carelessly. They are broken people in need of a Savior. I pray for their healing and salvation.
- Because You are the author and finisher of my faith, I will follow You, Jesus. You know the way to my eternal destination in heaven.

- I will live in confidence of Your plan for me, Father God. Your way is good and Your Holy Spirit is my counselor, guide, and comfort.

# Day 11

# East and West

*As far as the east is from the west, so far has He removed our transgressions from us* (Psalm 103:12).

While we've talked a lot about time and redemption, if we're going to be true to the continuum of space and time, we've got to look at Psalm 103.

Space. The final frontier! While man makes his feeble attempts to explore the great beyond our solar system, Jesus the Creator has put a truth right in front of us that should bring so much hope. When He laid everything out, He labeled it all with directions—north, south, east, and west.

Why would the Lord of All Things bother with directions in this backwater of the universe we call home? Because He's the ultimate architect. He plans, measures, weighs, and pulls out His plumb line to ensure everything is exact. The second reason Jesus gave us directions is because He hates for us to be lost—in every sense of the word. He's the God of the right path so He always wants us to know what that path is!

There's being lost as in "I took the wrong freeway exit and nothing looks familiar" and then there is *lost*—out of relationship, living in darkness, going in a direction that leads to destruction. That's why the Lord Jesus stamped our world with north, south, east, and west. Read Psalm 103:12 again.

Why would Jesus remove our sins "as far as the east is from the west"? While it is surely a reference to His bloodied arms stretched wide and nailed to a piece of wood as He laid down His life for us, looking through the lens of the time-space continuum, there is an eternal purpose for directions.

Suppose Jesus had removed our sins as far as the north is from the south. How far would that be? Exactly 12,406 miles. I put more miles on my car last year and so did you! The reason the Lord didn't remove our sins as far as the north is from the south is because that distance is finite. The poles are ending points and it wouldn't take much for us to go pick those sins right back up. Proverbs 26:11 compares it to a dog returning to his own vomit. Not a pretty picture, but that's what we do and God knows it.

So, just how far is the east from the west? As far as it gets. Think of two cars going in opposite directions. Will they meet again? No. There are no poles, no end points or finish lines. Jesus literally hurled our sins so far away that we could never retrieve them—ever. They are banished to the farthest reaches of space for all time and eternity, vanished when these amazing words are spoken: "Jesus, save me!"

Just like that, your past can be thrown to the farthest reaches of the universe never to haunt you again. All you have to do is invite Him to redeem it, to heal it, and remove the effects of it in your life today. It's really just as simple as saying, "Jesus save me," only you're saying, "Jesus, redeem this place of pain." He'll answer you. He's been waiting to answer that call from you from the very beginning of time!

And think of this—once time is finished, there is no space (see Rev. 10:7). It will all be gone—every sin and painful thing ever, forever. The plan is perfect.

> *Could it be any clearer that our former identity is now and forever deprived of its power? For we were co-crucified with Him to dismantle the stronghold of sin within us, so that we would not continue to live one moment longer submitted to sin's power* (Romans 6:6 TPT).

## I Declare in Jesus' Name...

- I am found by Jesus. I will never be lost again.
- My sins have been forgiven forever. I have faith in the blood of Jesus to redeem me.
- I will not pick up the bait of satan. I put all offenses behind me and refuse to revisit them.
- I refuse to watch reruns of my past. I will not dwell on my failures, hurts, and broken relationships any longer.
- I am in alignment for my assignment. I know Your plan for me is good and I will follow You.

*Day 12*

# Relational, Not Relative

*Jesus Christ is the same yesterday, today, and forever* (Hebrews 13:8).

How many times have you heard it said that something is "like clockwork"? It's meant as a compliment. That thing or person is looked at as reliable. Truth be told, time is anything but reliable.

With his Theory of Special Relativity, our friend Albert Einstein proved that time is relative to the observer, and it is. Five minutes on the shoulder of I-67 looking at flashing blue lights in my rearview mirror seems like an hour. An hour with my beautiful wife, Leanna, seems like it just started when she's kissing me goodbye.

Time is not stable—especially when it's not redeemed. In unredeemed time, everything is being lost. It's the times of your life when you're living for self and sin has you in its grip. Disorder and uncertainty mark your days and it seems like you can never win. You can never get ahead—everything is being lost or passing away. That, my friend, is because that is exactly what is happening. You're losing something because you are ruled by your past.

Now, here's the Good News—Jesus is stable. Unlike time, which is relative, He is Truth and Light. He is Life itself and He brings redemption into your timeline. When you apply King Jesus to your life, you apply redemption so that your past no longer pulls you backward. Jesus immediately turns your darkness into sunshine. Your downward spiral turns into an upward spiral. Instead, your future is inviting you forward.

> *You keep every promise you've ever made to me! Since your love for me is constant and endless, I ask you, Lord, to finish every good thing that you've begun in me* (Psalm 138:8 TPT).

So, because Jesus is so stable—so constant—He never changes. He is trustworthy. His Word, His promises, and His original intent for your life can be accessed in their fullness when you make Jesus the King of your life. Jesus is relational, not relative. You can trust in Him.

## I Declare in Jesus' Name...

- I trust in the name of Jesus. He is the Alpha, the Omega, Beginning and the End (see Rev. 22:13).
- Time is created by Jesus. It is subject to Him in every way.

- I repent of sin and selfishness. I no longer partner with unredeemed time.

- I am not ruled by my past. I am moving forward because Jesus is my Redeemer.

- Jesus is the One who was, who is, and who is to come. He is the Almighty—the ruler of my past, present, and future (see Rev. 1:8).

# Along for the Ride

*Your eyes saw my substance, being yet unformed. And in Your book they all were written, the days fashioned for me, when as yet there were none of them* (Psalm 139:16).

Jesus is in your past, your present, and your future—all at the same time. Nothing is hidden from Him. The ultimate Author and Finisher of your faith story (see Heb. 12:2), He likes to write the end of the book first. As a matter of fact, I believe that before He uttered the words that created time, space, and matter, God Almighty looked out over time to the end of the story, and space to the edges of the universe, and worked His way back to the beginning.

I imagine He saw it all. Every celebration and every war. Every harvest and every famine. Every smile and every tear. Every newborn baby, first day of school, graduation, wedding, and funeral. He looked out over it all and said, *"Let there be."*

Because the Lord knows the end of the story—your story—nothing surprises or shocks Him. He doesn't have to change His plan or have a backup. But here's the kicker: He had a plan for you before you were born.

> *Who saved us and called us to a holy calling, not because of our works but because of his own purpose and grace, which he gave us in Christ Jesus before the ages began* (2 Timothy 1:9 ESV).
>
> *For we are His workmanship, created in Christ Jesus for good works, which God prepared beforehand that we should walk in them* (Ephesians 2:10).

*Beforehand* is God's crazy cool way of saying, "before time even began." My friend, this is a great big word on purpose and destiny. If you're going to walk yours out, it's going to take some supernatural skillsets of redeeming your timeline. Pining for the past, or being trapped by it, is the most common way we let the "in-a-me" limit us. It's the spirit of halt and it's a killer.

Halt keeps you from progressing. It keeps blessings from getting to you. You cannot advance. You feel stuck. Halt keeps you immature and out of timing. To be forty years old and acting like a teenager is not cute or endearing. It's a curse. The spirit of halt is a curse! Reverse the curse by redeeming those places in your past that have put the brakes on your life today. It's time to push the accelerator on your life because Jesus is along for the ride. He knows how to get you to your destination.

## I Declare in Jesus' Name...

- Jesus knew me before I was created. He has a plan for my life and it is good.
- The "in-a-me" is defeated. I refuse to partner with the curse of being out of timing.
- I reverse the curse of halt. My past has been paid for by the blood of Jesus. It says better things about my future because it redeems my past.
- Accelerated timelines and trajectory belong to me. I am progressing to new levels of maturity and revelation.
- I will walk out every step of my purpose and destiny. Because I follow Jesus, I will never be lost again.

*Day 14*

## White as Snow

*In Him we have redemption through His blood, the
forgiveness of sins, according to the riches of His grace*
(Ephesians 1:7).

Redemption is the single most wonderful and precious "thing"
in the created universe. Why? Because it is the spotless and pure
life of Jesus Christ (see Jude 1:24). It is the essence of His life,
and it was spent and poured out to pay the terrible price for your
filth so you would no longer be a slave to sin. But there's more.
Consider this about the blood of Jesus: His blood is the matter
that changes time and space.

Remember that time, space, and matter are in continuum.
If one exists, the others exist. It's the same with redemption.
There is unredeemed time where we are losing everything and
redeemed time where Jesus steps in, applies His blood—which
is incorruptible—and the tables turn. We actually begin to
gain everything.

*Knowing that you were not redeemed with corruptible things, like silver or gold, from your aimless conduct received by tradition from your fathers, but with the precious blood of Christ, as of a lamb without blemish and without spot* (1 Peter 1:18-19).

The Jews understand that the blood of an unblemished lamb makes them like that lamb—spotless. This is why the prophet Isaiah said the following:

*"Come now, and let us reason together," says the Lord, "though your sins are like scarlet, they shall be as white as snow; though they are red like crimson, they shall be as wool"* (Isaiah 1:18).

In the Jewish culture, this is a picture of taking a red piece of cloth and un-dyeing it. My friend, you cannot un-dye something. The only way to do this is by turning back the clock—redeeming time. While in the natural this is impossible, in the supernatural that's what the sacrificial lamb did for them. It turned back time, and that's what the blood of Jesus does for all of us who believe today.

If there are places in your life that feel marked by a scarlet letter—L for loser, A for addict, U for unloved, F for forgotten, S for sin-ridden (there's a whole alphabet to choose from)—let Jesus turn back the clock. Ask Him to let His blood un-dye that crimson stain and make you white as snow. He will, you know. All you have to do is ask.

## I Declare in Jesus' Name...

- The blood of Jesus is incorruptible. It is the life that makes me whole in every way.
- Your blood is the matter that transforms space and time. You are redeeming my timeline.
- Your blood has made me whole and clean. My sins are no longer scarlet but white as snow.
- I am forgiven and washed clean by the blood of the Lamb. I will no longer dwell on my history but look forward to my destiny.
- King Jesus, turn back the clock. Reset, restore, and bring restitution in the places where I have been in bondage. I am free, in Your name!

# What Are You Waiting For?

*Brethren, do not be children in understanding; however, in malice be babes, but in understanding be mature* (1 Corinthians 14:20).

What if God created everything in six days, no matter what you want to call a day, with a history attached to it?

If on the seventh day, you cut down a tree that was only two days old, wouldn't it have rings in it as if it had been there for hundreds of years? Wouldn't the stones in the river already be smooth as if they had been there for thousands of years? That's not hard to imagine because God puts a great big value on maturity. How do I know? The account of the Promised Land.

*So it shall be, when the Lord your God brings you into the land of which He swore to your fathers, to Abraham, Isaac, and Jacob, to give you large and beautiful cities which you did not build, houses full of all good things, which you did not fill, hewn-out wells which you did not dig, vineyards and olive trees which*

*you did not plant—when you have eaten and are full*
(Deuteronomy 6:10-11).

What an awesome promise! God sent the Israelites into a land that was already mature. Why? Because if they had to plow and plant, fell, and build an entire society from the ground up, it would have been decades before God would be able to deal with them on the issue at hand—ridding the land of the evil nations occupying the real estate He set aside for the Jewish people. God and the Jews had a relationship to rekindle and the Lord was not willing to waste any more time.

God's love of maturity is also seen in the stars. Wouldn't the light from the stars be immediately seen from earth on the fourth day? That means they would have a history of however many light years it would take for the light to get to our planet already attached.

Look at the first man and woman. When God breathed life into Adam as a grown man who could already stand on his very first day, wasn't his body created as if he had gone through years of learning to walk, talk, and think like a grown man? Eve was a mature woman from the moment God created her out of Adam's rib. He did not have to push her in a baby carriage. Why would the Lord create them fully developed? Relationship. He wanted an adult relationship with them and He did not want to wait.

That's why He wants to redeem your timeline. Relationship. He wants you full, whole, mature, prosperous, and living out your purpose and destiny with Him right now. What are you waiting for? He's already there waiting for you with arms wide open!

## I Declare in Jesus' Name...

- I do not want to waste any more time. Jesus, break off anything that is holding me back from right relationship with You.
- The broken things in my life are made whole by the sacrifice of Jesus. I am full and whole, not lacking in anything.
- My past belongs in Jesus' hands. His blood has redeemed the pain of my past so I am not limited today.
- I am loved by God the Father, Jesus the Son, and the Holy Spirit. They are working all things in my timeline for my good because I love God and am called according to His purpose.

*Day 16*

# Find Your Seat, Please!

*Even when we were dead in trespasses, made us alive together with Christ (by grace you have been saved), and raised us up together, and made us sit together in the heavenly places in Christ Jesus* (Ephesians 2:5-6).

Our God hung the sun, the moon, and flung all the stars across the vast sky that we look at every night. There's nothing He can't do. Because God is outside of time and not subject to it, He can also step in and out of your timeline any place He wants to. Right now, He can be with you at the moment of your birth or even while you were being formed—like He did with Jeremiah.

*Before I formed you in the womb I knew you; before you were born I sanctified you* (Jeremiah 1:5).

This very minute, God can be with you as you read this and be present in the last few moments of your life. Why would He do that? To make sure your death glorifies Him. He did this with Peter in John 21:19 when Jesus told him by what death he would glorify God. Jesus was telling Peter, "I've been there and seen your finish. I know how this story goes and your death is going to glorify Me, Peter." All the while, He was with Peter in his "right now."

Just like that, Paul says those who are saved are already counted among the citizens of heaven and "seated in heavenly places."

How can you be seated in heavenly places at the same time you are reading this devotion? Because in God's eternal view of your life, He sees it all at the same time just like a helicopter hovering 1,000 feet above a train sees the engine, the caboose, and every car in between. Like Peter, He's telling you, "I see you today, but I also see your end and it glorifies Me. You did it! You're going to make it, so keep going."

Can I tell you something you might think is a little crazy? I've already prayed and asked God to be with me in my final minutes. I've asked Him to let me feel His manifest presence in a way that comforts and strengthens me. I want to be a faithful witness with a rock-solid testimony of a redeemed life right up until my last breath on earth and my first breath of heaven's fresh air.

I would encourage you to do the same. Take your seat in that heavenly place and ask Jesus to travel into your future. Ask Him to apply His amazing redemptive blood to your final moments so they not only glorify Him to those around you, they will also leave a lasting legacy of redemption and blessing for a thousand generations to come.

*Therefore know that the Lord your God, He is God, the faithful God who keeps covenant and mercy for a thousand generations with those who love Him and keep His commandments* (Deuteronomy 7:9).

## I Declare in Jesus' Name...

- The Lord is outside of time. He sees my beginning, end, and every moment in between.

- Jesus is a time traveler. He can and does go into any moment in my timeline I ask Him to.

- Redemption is the reason Jesus travels through time. I trust Him with my yesterday, today, and tomorrow.

- My last minutes will glorify You, Jesus. I proclaim strength and faith as I step into eternity with You.

- Because of the manifest presence of Jesus, my end will be a new beginning for multitudes.

# A Prayer for Works
# of Redemption

*Father God, You thought of everything! Before You said, "Let there be," You had a plan of redemption in place for Your creation. You knew man would fall, but You loved us and wanted a family so much that You even called us "very good." Thank You, Lord, that anything good in me is because of You.*

*I want to be an open book to You, Holy Spirit. I know You have written my story and You know the end from the beginning. You are truly the author and finisher of my faith. I invite You to go behind me to spare me from the harm of my past and go before me to lead me to my forever destiny with You. I trust You, Lord.*

*Jesus, Your blood has redeemed me. It has turned the stains of my sin as white as snow. Thank You for throwing my sins as far as the east is from the west and not keeping a record of my wrongs. I repent of keeping that record on my own. I do not want the guilt, shame,* and baggage of past trespasses—mine and those against me. I surrender them to You, Jesus. Redeem them so they are no longer a curse to my today or my tomorrow.

I love You and ask You to speak to me in dreams and prophetic encounters. Draw me to You in a new relationship as I follow Your plan for my Kingdom destiny. Thank You for always loving me no matter what. Amen.

Then I said, "Behold, I come; in the scroll of the book it is written of me. I delight to do Your will, O my God, and Your law is within my heart" (Psalm 40:7-8).

So I said, "Here I am! I'm coming to you as a sacrifice, for in the prophetic scrolls of your book you have written about me. I delight to fulfill your will, my God, for your living words are written upon the pages of my heart" (Psalm 40:7-8 TPT).

# The Power of Redemption

It's the central theme of the entire Bible. It's what Jesus Christ came to bring and who He Himself became—redemption.

> Redemption is the act of buying something back or paying a price or ransom to return something to your possession. Redemption is the English translation of the Greek word *agorazo,* meaning "to purchase in the marketplace." In ancient times, it often referred to the act of buying a slave. It carried the meaning of freeing someone from chains, prison, or slavery. —JACK ZAVADA

**Premise 3: Redemption changes everything—not just over time but for all time.**

Redemption has the power to change all creation. It's what happens when Jesus shows up. He literally is our redemption. He changes everything within that time—including space and matter—from a curse to a blessing.

Redemption also changes lost people to family, hated people to celebrated, and wicked people to holy. Redemption changes leprous bodies to perfect human specimens. Redemption brings enslaved people into freedom and transforms dead things into living things.

Through the transformational power of redemption, messed-up minds become gifted learners, and shameful, pitiful people become honored and confident. I cannot tell you how much I love redemption because it changes ownership. When things move from the Kingdom of hell to the Kingdom of heaven, the King of Kings gets to have dominion and His will on earth as it is in heaven.

His blood and His love are the currency that pays the price of real life and transformation.

> *Those who trust in their wealth and boast in the multitude of their riches, none of them can by any means redeem his brother, nor give to God a ransom for him—for the redemption of their souls is costly, and it shall cease forever—that he should continue to live eternally, and not see the Pit* (Psalm 49:6-9).

*Day 17*

# Goodness and Mercy
# Shall Follow

*Surely goodness and mercy shall follow me all the days of my life; and I will dwell in the house of the Lord forever* (Psalm 23:6).

Psalm 23 is something else! Not only does King David pen a passionate piece of poetry, he puts the entirety of our human existence into the proverbial "nutshell" and it all starts with "The Lord is my Shepherd."

That makes us the sheep and, let me tell you, that's not a compliment. Sheep are dumb. Laugh if you want, but I'm a lifelong Texan who grew up on a ranch. Calling sheep dumb is actually being nice. If there were ever an animal that needed care and protection, it's sheep. Why? They have a tendency to not only get lost, but to walk right into danger without a thought in their tiny brains that this thing might not end well.

You and I are so like sheep! King David knew it. Being the knucklehead boy he was, he'd gotten himself into some pretty hairy scrapes over the years. It started with bears and lions, graduated to giants, and eventually led to entire armies of enemies, harems of honeys, and kids with all kinds of daddy issues.

With all that, David knew where his help came from—the Shepherd. He knew where to find still waters, green pastures, and restoration for his soul. He experienced safety in places that will kill you and even had supernatural health poured over his head. King David ran to the place at the table where the Shepherd could feed him, love him, and forgive him for all the hell he'd broken loose in his own life and the lives of those he never wanted to hurt, but did. This, my friends, is called a testimony.

And at the end of it all, David says the most amazing thing: "Surely goodness and mercy will follow me all the days of my life." Let's do this prophetic poem justice and look at it in *The Passion Translation*.

> *So why would I fear the future? Only goodness and tender love pursue me all the days of my life. Then afterward, when my life is through, I'll return to your glorious presence to be forever with you!* (Psalm 23:6)

Very aware of his "right now" and his tendency to make a huge mess, David declared his future secure. How? Because he had seen the way the goodness and mercy of God had followed behind him and cleaned up those messes of his past. While those things hurt at the time and had some very real consequences, redemption had been applied because David always ran right to the Shepherd every time he lost his way.

Do you run to the Good Shepherd? He wants to give you a home and a future in His family. All you have to do is let redemption—goodness and mercy—follow you all the days of your life.

## I Declare in Jesus' Name...

- Jesus is my Good Shepherd. His rod fights off my enemies and His staff draws me into His presence.
- The Lord gives me good things, provides for me, and calls me family in the presence of those who call me a curse.
- My mess does not rule over me. Jesus has brought redemption and changed my curses into blessings.
- Goodness and mercy follow me all the days of my life because Jesus is a time traveler. He brings redemption into my past to fulfill my future.

# Day 18

# The Issachar Anointing

*The sons [of the tribe] of Issachar who had understanding of the times, to know what Israel ought to do* (1 Chronicles 12:32).

Imagine, if you will, having the wisdom and supernatural insight to know what do to in any situation, at any time. Being in the right place at the right time, every time. Never early. Never late. Never missing out. Always on time.

The Bible tells us of a tribe of people that God blessed with a gift for timing. The sons of Issachar were a large tribe of men skilled in battle. Because of their wisdom and knack for being in sync with God, the nation's leaders would inquire of them in matters of state, finance, war, and God's calendar.

When kings and generals don't make a move without consulting you first, that's called influence and it's a really big deal.

Just like the sons of Issachar, Daniel was a timing freak. He walked in prophetic favor with three of the most powerful kings on earth. An isolated outsider in a foreign land, the key to

Daniel's gifts of dream interpretation, words of knowledge, and prophetic timing was his supernatural intimacy with the Lord. He actually knew God as the "Ancient of Days," which means "older than time."

In supernatural sync with His heart, the Lord not only trusted Daniel with wisdom, insight, and understanding for earthly kings, He trusted him with the prophetic timing of the earthly appearance of the King of Kings.

> *I was watching in the night visions, and behold, One like the Son of Man, coming with the clouds of heaven! He came to the Ancient of Days, and they brought Him near before Him* (Daniel 7:13).

As the second in command of all Babylon and the chief of the Chaldeans—astrologers or "wise men"—Daniel told these men of a God who was above all gods. He taught these pagan magicians to scan the heavens for the star that would lead them to the greatest King of all, Jesus.

Four hundred years later, Daniel's gift of timing translated into gifts of gold, frankincense, and myrrh that sustained the Son of God and His family for at least 12 years. That's the power of the Issachar anointing!

## I Declare in Jesus' Name...

- The anointing for perfect timing belongs to me. I walk in the Issachar anointing for times and seasons.

- Father God has given me supernatural wisdom and insight, understanding and knowledge. I have a clear vision of my future.
- I am a person of excellence. I stand in the presence of kings and not unknown men.
- Prophetic dreams, visions, words of knowledge, and interpretation are mine. They are gifts of favor to point people to Jesus.

*Day 19*

# All Means All

*And we know that all things work together for good to those who love God, to those who are the called according to His purpose* (Romans 8:28).

When it comes to the subject of redeeming your timeline, Romans 8:28 really floats my boat. When it says "all things work together for good to those who love God," just know that "all" really does mean all, and that includes your past.

"But Pastor Troy, you don't understand the bad things that have happened to me. I didn't deserve it but I live with the memories. They are painful open wounds. I just can't get past the abuses I've suffered."

My friend, I do understand—more than you know—and I can tell you this: You can be healed and made whole from the pain and devastation of evil done against you in your past. Let me tell you, I know from experience the difference between bruises and scars.

Bruises are places where you bleed on the inside. People may not be able to see your pain, but you feel it with every breath. These become open wounds the more you talk and dwell on them. If you don't get healed, this open wound will define you as a victim.

God's not a liar when He says He works all things for our good. He can take something awful—a curse—and make something beautiful and blessed. He can change your bruises and open wounds into scars. Scars are what happens when healing and redemption enter the scene. Warriors have scars. Overcomers and victors have scars. They can say, "That was then, but this is now." Victims cannot say that.

Just ask Jacob. It was a curse on him to go into the wedding tent and find his wife was not his beautiful Rachel but her cross-eyed sister, Leah. He lost another seven years of his life as an indentured servant to his father-in-law to finally get Rachel.

It was a curse for Leah to be married to a man who didn't love her and likely treated her more like a plaything than a wife. It was a curse to be in competition every day with Rachel. Leah obviously resented Rachel's intrusion into her marriage. But in the grand scheme of God's handiwork, the children Jacob and Leah had together—Reuben, Simeon, Levi, Judah, Issachar, and Zebulun—account for six of the twelve tribes of Israel.

Do you see it? The blessings of God and the promise of a messiah-redeemer came through Leah's bloodline, not Rachel's. Jesus is a direct descendant of Judah, which means "praise." Judah's brother, Issachar, is the dude whose descendants are known for the blessing of supernatural timing. When I tell you all means all, I really mean it!

When you ask Jesus to go back into your timeline to the painful places that have not healed despite years and years of trying to forgive and forget, He will. He's just waiting for you to let go and let Him redeem that wound.

> *If I fly with wings into the shining dawn, you're there!*
> *If I fly into the radiant sunset, you're there waiting!*
> (Psalm 139:9 TPT)

He's literally waiting. Are you willing?

## I Declare in Jesus' Name...

- My timeline belongs to Jesus. I invite Him to apply redemption to the places of deepest hurt.
- The pain and shame of my past is gone. It has been redeemed by the blood of Jesus.
- I no longer have bruises. My wounds have healed. I am not a victim but a victor.
- The scars of my past are a great testimony of Jesus. He is my healer and redeemer.

- I am not defined by my past. I am an overcomer. Jesus has a white stone with a new name for me in heaven (see Rev. 2:17).

*Day 20*

# The Days the Locusts Have Eaten

*So I will restore to you the years that the swarming locust has eaten, the crawling locust, the consuming locust, and the chewing locust, My great army which I sent among you* (Joel 2:25).

Because we don't live in the Middle East or Africa, you and I really have no clue the damage locusts are capable of. When they swarm in on the desert winds, those in their path are terrified. They know every green and living thing is about to be devoured. Life swallowed up by a swarm of death.

That's what it means when the locusts have "eaten" your days, months, and years. The time has been swallowed by death. All is lost. No going back, and moving forward has become more than difficult.

Isn't that how we feel about our failures and broken relationships? Or the injustices done to us and those we've dealt to others? You cannot erase your past any more than you can get your crop back from the insect horde. It's impossible! Or is it?

*But Jesus looked at them and said to them, "With men this is impossible, but with God all things are possible"* (Matthew 19:26).

We know "all" means *all* and we know from Romans 8:28 that God is working all things for our good. When the Lord says He will restore the time you've lost, He doesn't reverse time. He gives new opportunity to walk out what was missed.

A good example is my friend and her daughter. When she was young, the daughter was savagely bullied. Innocent and alone, she could not fathom the injustice. No amount of love and affirmation from her parents could ease the pain. Counseling was fruitless. Prayer and forgiveness were applied and taken back time and time again. Despite all my friend's efforts to help her daughter, the wounds were too deep and the pain was too great to let go.

For years, that little girl suffered as a victim. No victory, only loss. She became a bitter, angry teenager, quick to blame others for her problems. Her favorite target was the one who loved her the most—her mama. The one who championed her, fought for her, dried her tears, prayed and prophesied life into her was the one she punished for her pain.

Let me tell you, my friend's life was a nightmare of wanting to love her daughter and have a healthy relationship with a whole and healed child but never being able to. Then a pastor's wife prayed a simple prayer over my friend that changed everything.

*Lord, restore the days the locusts have eaten between my sweet friend and her daughter. They've been stolen and devoured by the enemy, but we believe You will return them seven times over. Give them new opportunities for a deeper and stronger relationship. Do this for the glory of Your name.*

Without knowing it, they had prayed for Jesus to redeem their timeline, and He showed up in a mighty way. He not only restored that little girl's identity and purpose, their relationship is renewed beyond anything my friend expected. Take that, devil from hell!

*The thief does not come except to steal, and to kill, and to destroy. I have come that they may have life, and that they may have it more abundantly* (John 10:10).

What have the locusts eaten in your life? What has been taken that you want returned? Ask Jesus to redeem it and don't be surprised if He gives back the time the enemy has stolen in abundance!

## I Declare in Jesus' Name...

- I am a life breather, not a death breather. I will speak blessings instead of curses over myself and others.
- Lord, give back the years the locusts have eaten. I forgive all injustice done to me and proclaim victory over places of defeat.

- My times are in Your hands, Lord. I ask You to restore, renew, and bring restitution for the days I've lost to guilt, shame, and the pain of my past. I am free!

- My pain is in my past. It no longer has the power to control me because it has been redeemed by the blood of Jesus. My wounds are healed!

- New opportunities and renewed relationships are coming to me. The Lord is replacing dead dreams and relationships with life more abundant.

# A Mere Moment

*For a thousand years in Your sight are like yesterday when it is past, and like a watch in the night* (Psalm 90:4).

Like I said earlier in this book, time was created by God. He is not subject to it. He can move in and out of it at will, but He does not live in time. We do. God lives in a place where there is no time, space, or matter. He calls it both eternity and everlasting.

*I have been established from everlasting, from the beginning, before there was ever an earth* (Proverbs 8:23).

In everlasting, there is no space because there is no such thing as time. As soon as God has a thought, it becomes. That's the omnipotence of God—His power to create in less than an instant. Likewise, when He decides to move, He's already there. That's called the omnipresence of the Lord. He can be everywhere at one time because He's not subject to space and time.

That is why the Bible reminds us to be patient. When we are overwhelmed by today, God is not bothered at all. He sees the big picture.

> *But, beloved, do not forget this one thing, that with the Lord one day is as a thousand years, and a thousand years as one day* (2 Peter 3:8).

In God's eternal eyes, your life doesn't even equal a day, much less an hour of a day. James 4:14 says our lives are "but a vapor" in God's everlasting scheme of things. Man is a mere moment in millennia. While it sounds like we are insignificant, the Word says we are anything but.

> *But did He not make them one, having a remnant of the Spirit? And why one? He seeks godly offspring* (Malachi 2:15).

What does it mean that the Lord desires godly offspring? It means God created man to be His family—His sons and daughters. He is a good Father and He has a heavenly home for us. Knowing that, consider this: If our lives are a moment here, how much more life is ours in heaven? With no time to limit us, our destination greatly exceeds our current habitation.

While this life is important, it is the dress rehearsal for the real life and transformation that is outside of time. Are you prepared? Are you dressed for the occasion? And have you studied your script—the Bible? Have you met the director? Don't be so caught up in today that you miss the millennia!

## I Declare in Jesus' Name...

- My times are in the hands of the Lord. I trust Him to lead me to my expected end.
- My life is but a puff of smoke. I will make the most of it by living for Jesus and bringing many into the Kingdom of God.
- Eternity is my destination. I am redeemed by the blood of Jesus.
- My generations belong to the Lord. Because I love Him and am called according to His purpose, I will see a thousand of my generations living in eternity.
- I am in alignment for my Kingdom assignment and dressed for the occasion. The Lord is directing my footsteps.

# The Curse of Halt

*Then he said to me, "Do not fear, Daniel, for from the first day that you set your heart to understand, and to humble yourself before your God, your words were heard; and I have come because of your words. But the prince of the kingdom of Persia withstood me twenty-one days; and behold, Michael, one of the chief princes, came to help me, for I had been left alone there with the kings of Persia" (Daniel 10:12-13).*

Have you ever prayed for the Lord to intervene in a situation and you didn't see that He did? Have you asked for His help, favor, an answer to a question, or a dream within your life to come true, and you find yourself still waiting? I have. And I'm pretty sure we all have.

While we are the ones subject to time, not God, there are times His answers to our prayers get held up. They did for Daniel. Read Daniel chapter 10. He had a vision of the future that was so confusing and terrifying that he couldn't eat for three weeks. Finally, he's standing on the banks of the Tigris River between modern-day Iraq and Iran, and a man with "a face like lightning and eyes like flaming torches" appeared before him.

While this heavenly being doesn't give a name, it's apparent he is a bad motor scooter. It's also apparent from his glowing frame that he stands in the presence of God and carries the Word of the Lord. He's so overwhelming that Daniel flat passes out! The heavenly being has to touch him and stand him back up before saying something curious.

"God heard you the very first day you prayed and He sent me to bring the answer, but the evil principality over the place you live has delayed the answer for three weeks."

That is what I call a spirit of halt. This curse stops the promises of God in your life and it keeps you from progressing. Here, it's a territorial spirit over a pagan nation and it is strong! God's messenger not only battles his way there, after 21 days the biggest, baddest angelic being ever created, the archangel Michael, had to step in so the message could get through. If I had to guess why, I would look at this verse:

> *Soon I will return to fight against the prince of Persia, and when I go, the prince of Greece will come; but first I will tell you what is written in the Book of Truth. (No one supports me against them except Michael, your prince)* (Daniel 10:20-21 NIV).

My friend, timing can get held up by the demonic. Man gave satan authority over this realm and we have a responsibility to pray the answers through. Notice the angelic being said, "No one supports me against them except Michael." God answered Daniel's prayer on the first day; the answers came after 21 days of prayer and fasting by one man. Long before Daniel's angelic visitation, David experienced this very same spirit of halt in his life.

> *The Lord confides in those who fear him; he makes his covenant known to them. My eyes are ever on the Lord, for only he will release my feet from the snare* (Psalm 25:14-15 NIV).

There were many times in his life when David felt like his feet were in a snare and he could not move forward. Being a man after God's own heart, he ran to God for help, but we know from the Psalms that the answers didn't always come right away. Still, David never gave up praying.

Have you given up on the answers to your prayers? Are there prayers you no longer pray—prayers for financial freedom, the salvation of a loved one, or for direction in your purpose and destiny? I tell you, my friend, do not give up! Do not stop! Your redemption draws near.

Your breakthrough is coming, but like Daniel and David, you have to continue to battle in prayer. Gather intercessors and prayer partners to join you. The prince of the power of the air (see Eph. 2:2), satan, wants to keep you under the spirit of halt. Empower God's angel armies with your petitions and destroy demonic delay!

## I Declare in Jesus' Name...

- My eyes are ever on the Lord. I run into His presence as a fleeing man runs into a strong tower for protection.
- My prayers and petitions are powerful. They have reached the ear of the Lord and His messengers are on their way.
- I will not give up on the Lord! He is answering my prayers and will not leave me empty-handed!
- I partner with the armies of heaven to break the spirit of halt over my life. No demonic principality will hold them back or hold me down.
- The snare of the enemy has been broken. I have been made mighty for the pulling down of strongholds, the casting down of evil imaginations, and every high thing that exalts itself against the knowledge of God.

# Mud in Your Eye

*When He had said these things, He spat on the ground and made clay with the saliva; and He anointed the eyes of the blind man with the clay. And He said to him, "Go, wash in the pool of Siloam" (which is translated, Sent). So he went and washed, and came back seeing* (John 9:6-7).

Jesus and the disciples are walking in Jerusalem when they come upon a man blind from birth. The disciples are curious, as are we. They make some assumptions, as do we.

*Rabbi, who sinned, this man or his parents, that he was born blind?* (John 9:2)

What they are really asking is the same thing we ask today when we see the lame, blind, or disabled: "What did they do to deserve that, God?" Admit it. It's crossed your mind just as it crossed the disciples'. At the root of this, we are questioning the goodness of God. Then Jesus sets them, and us, straight.

*Jesus answered, "Neither this man nor his parents sinned, but that the works of God should be revealed in him"* (John 9:3).

What Jesus is saying is that God made this man blind on purpose and He did it for His purpose. To find out why, let's go back in time to the Sinai Peninsula where a once-powerful prince-turned-shepherd is talking with God Almighty on a patch of holy ground.

*Then Moses said to the Lord, "O my Lord, I am not eloquent, neither before nor since You have spoken to Your servant; but I am slow of speech and slow of tongue." So the Lord said to him, "Who has made man's mouth? Or who makes the mute, the deaf, the seeing, or the blind? Have not I, the Lord?"* (Exodus 4:10-11)

God freely admits to Moses that He makes those man sees as broken for His purpose—which is always His glory. Everything God does is to bring glory and honor to Himself. The Lord is actually pleased to make those we consider incomplete to point to Him and say, "My life glorifies God."

This blind beggar on the streets of Jerusalem was about to glorify God and he didn't have a clue! If he asked to be healed, the record doesn't show it. The disciples point, Jesus kneels. He spits on the ground and makes a handful of mud. He then rubs it on this man's face and says, "Go wash in the pool of Siloam."

I don't know about you, but I find this offensive. Spit and mud? Is Jesus for real? How is this man supposed to find the pool? He's blind, for heaven's sake! Are you kidding me!?

Well, it's a good thing this man was not offended because he got right up, found his way to the pool, and came back without the help of a guide dog. Everyone was stunned and they should be, because scholars believe this man was born without eyeballs in those sockets.

Why mud? Because man was fashioned from the dust of the earth. God breathed the breath of life into Adam and he became a living soul (see Gen. 2:7). Just like that, Jesus grabbed some dirt, spat some supernatural saliva on it, and, turning back time, formed some eyeballs for this man. Sending him to the pool was an act of baptism, or redemption, that screams, "I Am the living water! You will never thirst—or wander around in the dark—again."

In His kindness, God turns back time to the very beginning and says, "It's time for you to glorify Me. People will see My goodness pass before them every time they look in your eyes from this day forward." My friend, this is what redemption looks like. Here's to mud in your eye!

## I Declare in Jesus' Name...

- **The Lord is my healer. Jesus' blood has paid it all and the Lord is redeeming my health.**

- My life will glorify the Lord. I will point to Him and Him only.
- I will not partner with offense. The Lord works in mysterious ways and I will praise the outcome of His handiwork.
- I am fearfully and wonderfully made. Jesus loves me and created me to glorify Him.
- The Lord Jehovah Nissi is on my battlefield. My healer will redeem and restore me to testify to His goodness.

*Day 24*

# Pawns of Predestination?

*And the Lord God commanded the man, saying, "Of every tree of the garden you may freely eat; but of the tree of the knowledge of good and evil you shall not eat, for in the day that you eat of it you shall surely die"* (Genesis 2:16-17).

Free will is the greatest gift God bestowed on mankind. "But Pastor Troy, what about redemption? Isn't that the greatest gift because it leads to eternal life?"

While redemption is crazy cool and the backbone of this book, free will is even more basic than redemption. Free will makes love possible. Without free will there is no love because a gift that's demanded is not a gift. It has to be given and accepted freely. And without love, free will is useless, like the clanging gong of First Corinthians 13.

What I'm saying is free will and love make redemption possible. Now, let's jump off into the deep end and talk about a very controversial topic that has free will at the core—predestination.

*And we know that all things work together for good to those who love God, to those who are the called according to His purpose. For whom He foreknew, He also predestined to be conformed to the image of His Son, that He might be the firstborn among many brethren. Moreover whom He predestined, these He also called; whom He called, these He also justified; and whom He justified, these He also glorified* (Romans 8:28-30).

God working all things for our good has a lot to do with God forgiving, forgetting, and redeeming time. But what does it mean to be "called according to His purpose"? To be "foreknown" and "predestined?" I'm glad you asked.

The verb *predestine* is the Greek word *prohorizo*, which is made up of two words—*pro*, which means "in front" or "before," and *horizo,* which means "to determine, ordain or appoint." Its original meaning was "setting a boundary" or "to separate." The word *horizon* is clearly from this definition as it's the boundary of how far we can see, right?

*Prohorizo* also means to lay claim to something in a contractual dispute of property or money. Keep that in mind.

Because it is associated with election and foreknowledge, the definition of *predestine* in our 21st-century Western mindset can be extremely rigid. As a matter of fact, most Christians believe it means God plays favorites. He picks and chooses those He loves and those He doesn't—those He will save and those He will not. My friend, that is a very cruel God and not the God of the Bible.

If your future is set in stone and all your days are rigidly predestined, why does God ponder the ways of man?

> *For the ways of man are before the eyes of the Lord, and He ponders all his paths* (Proverbs 5:21).

You see, being "predestined" does not make you a puppet with every word you speak, step you take, and move you make being planned and executed by the master pulling the strings. That flies in the face of free will. If our God is love—and He is according to First John 4:7—free will is a major part of His character. It's literally who He is. You, being made in His image, were given free will to choose to love Him or not. The *not* comes with some pretty painful consequences.

Our strict view of predestination makes God into an eternal chess master pushing pawns around a game called life. It is also lazy theology for Christians who don't want to take responsibility for their actions or outcomes. "God willed it." "I was supposed to be here today." "It's all part of God's plan." "If God wants it to happen, it will. If He doesn't, it won't." Have you said any of these things?

Now, those last words are in the Bible. They are, and they are spoken by a Pharisee named Gamaliel in Acts 5:39, who was an enemy of God and persecutor of Jesus. He utters these words to wash his hands of any responsibility for the outcome of his decisions, same as we do today.

"If they're meant to live they will. God will feed them. I don't have to."

"If they're meant to get saved, it will happen. Nothing I say will matter."

The doctrine of predestination says we don't have to be responsible for our actions, words, and decisions because God is directing it all. That's a lie straight from the pit of hell. Heck! Could Judas have repented and not sold Jesus out? Yes. How do I know? Jesus gave him the moneybag "knowing he was a thief." He gave Judas a chance to turn away from the devil and his evil agenda every single day. Judas remained a thief despite Jesus' hope he would choose better—His hope Judas would choose Him.

My friend, God is outside of time. He created time and, as I've pointed out numerous times in these pages, He "knows the end from the beginning." The end—your end—is so important to our heavenly Father that He looked out over space and time, saw it all, wrote in all our books then said, "Let there be light." If He knows the end of the story, as Psalm 139:16 says, He also knows the choices you made before you make them, including your choice to love and serve Him for eternity.

When it comes to *prohorizo*, Jesus the Creator has been beyond the horizon. He's seen past the boundary of space, time, sin, and death. What did He see there? You. Lost, alone, and separated from Him. He looked the devil in the eye and said, "*Prohorizo!* This one is legally Mine. They belong to Me by the covenant of My blood and the contract of free will. They have chosen Me."

So, when you see the words *predestined, willed, called, foreknew, determined beforehand*, and *elected*, remember—you are not a robot. You are a living soul filled with the Spirit of the Living God (see Gen. 2:7). You serve a God of love who created you with an ability to decide. Sadly, many, like Judas, don't choose Him, but that's not you!

> *But as for me and my house, we will serve the Lord* (Joshua 24:15).

You are responsible for your life. You are not a pawn on a chess board and God is not an evil puppet master in the sky. Use your free will to bring the love of God to those who need to know He is writing their story and they get to choose the ending!

## I Declare in Jesus' Name...

- God is good. He is a God of love and I can trust Him with my past, present, and future.
- God knows my end and calls it good. I will glorify Him to my last breath.
- My sins are forgiven and my past is redeemed. I am whole. The devil's lies cannot touch me.

- I am chosen because I have chosen to love the One True God. He is the author and finisher of my faith.
- As for me and my house, we shall serve the Lord.

# A Prayer for Great Works of Redemption

*Father God, You thought of everything before You spoke the words, "Let there be light..." You looked out over time and space and You saw it all—good and bad—before You called forth time. Still, You said it was "good." You call me and my life "good." Thank You, God, for prophesying into me before I was even born.*

*Lord, give me a supernatural grace and an Issachar anointing to be in perfect sync with Your heart and Your timing. The tribe of Issachar were men who understood times, seasons, and Your heart in them. They knew "what Israel ought to do." Lord, I declare that anointing on me. I pray I would always be at the right place, at the right time for the right miracle to happen.*

*Just like the sons of Issachar, I proclaim the wisdom of Your timing and the influence it brings. Let me give godly insight and understanding to kings and those in authority for positive Kingdom outcomes. Let my words be a beacon of light to those in darkness and of hope to those in the valley of trial.*

*I thank You for redeeming my timeline. Expose any word or action from my past that needs Your supernatural grace and redemption. I will gladly bring it to the Cross so You can reverse the curse in my life and make it a blessing for generations to come. Amen.*

*The sons* [of the tribe] *of Issachar who had under-standing of the times, to know what Israel ought to do* (1 Chronicles 12:32).

# Redemption Changes Everything!

If you can believe God can be with somebody on the other side of the world at the same time He is with you, it is not much of a leap to believe He can step into your past even though He is with you right now. The continuum is one of the most amazing features of all God's creation, and Jesus Christ rules and reigns over all of it.

> *In the beginning was the Word, and the Word was with God, and the Word was God. He was in the beginning with God. All things were made through Him, and without Him nothing was made that was made* (John 1:1-3).

Before He came to earth as the man Jesus, the Bible says His name in eternity was "the Word." According to this scripture passage, Jesus can put His hands on time because God (the Word) spoke the universe into existence. As its Creator, all of the universe belongs to Him and is in His control.

*Ah, Sovereign Lord, you have made the heavens and the earth by your great power and outstretched arm. Nothing is too hard for you* (Jeremiah 32:17 NIV).

He literally orders time along with space and matter because He is the Prince of Peace.

*For God is not a God of disorder, but of peace—as in all the congregations of the Lord's people* (1 Corinthians 14:33 NIV).

As we'll find out in this section, Jesus can stop time, accelerate it, reverse it, and manipulate it in any way He wants. Along with that, He can change space and distance because it is in continuum with time. He can change matter just like when Jesus turned water into wine and healed people of leprosy. Again, time, space, and matter, though different, are totally inseparable. This is where God can jump out of your box and become all you need Him to be—no matter the time!

**Premise 4: You can introduce redemption into any part of your timeline and it changes everything within the timeline, including space and matter.**

This is going to be fun!

# Redemption Changes Matter

*By that will we have been sanctified through the offering of the body of Jesus Christ once for all. And every priest stands ministering daily and offering repeatedly the same sacrifices, which can never take away sins. But this Man [Jesus Christ], after He had offered one sacrifice for sins forever, sat down at the right hand of God* (Hebrews 10:10-12).

The redemption of Jesus Christ dealt with the problem of sin "once for all." All means all—past, present, and future. His sacrifice for sins interrupts and changes how the rules work in time. It is one redemption for all time for all sin.

> [Jesus] *gave himself for us, that he might redeem us from all iniquity* (Titus 2:14 KJV).

Jesus Christ redeemed us "from all iniquity," and He obtained it by ransoming Himself for us. When eternal redemption enters into time and space, the very history of time is changed, both spiritual and natural. As a matter of fact, redemption changes matter. Let's look at Matthew's account of how Jesus brought redemption into physical matter—in this case, the body of a brother who couldn't move his body.

> *So He got into a boat, crossed over, and came to His own city. Then behold, they brought to Him a paralytic lying on a bed. When Jesus saw their faith, He said to the paralytic, "Son, be of good cheer; your sins are forgiven you"* (Matthew 9:1-2).

By faith, they gained access to the forgiveness of sins. Redemption changes a sinner into a saint. Jesus has entered into the picture and now all is forgiven. This is going to be a problem with the onlooking religious people.

> *And at once some of the scribes said within themselves, "This Man blasphemes!" But Jesus, knowing their thoughts, said, "Why do you think evil in your hearts? For which is easier, to say, 'Your sins are forgiven you,' or to say, 'Arise and walk'?"* (Matthew 9:3-5)

Did you catch it? Jesus is saying they are the same. The power to forgive (change time) is the same power to heal (change matter) because they are all in continuum. If your sins can be forgiven, and they can, then your physical body can also be healed. The muscles can grow, the nerves can connect, and suddenly you are dancing instead of being carried.

Jesus might as well have said, "Which is easier, to forgive sins or change the physical properties of matter?" For Him, they are equally easy. For us, they are equally needed.

## I Declare in Jesus' Name...

- Redemption changes both spiritual and natural. Time and matter are in continuum.
- The ability to forgive sins changes time. The power to heal changes matter. Through the Holy Spirit, I walk in the power of redemption.
- Jesus is healing my physical body. His blood has authority for all time, in all space, and over all matter.
- There is one redemption for all sin for all time. I am forgiven and fully redeemed.

_Day 26_

# Supernaturally Transformed

_Then He commanded the multitudes to sit down on the grass. And He took the five loaves and the two fish, and looking up to heaven, He blessed and broke and gave the loaves to the disciples; and the disciples gave to the multitudes. So they all ate and were filled, and they took up twelve baskets full of the fragments that remained_ (Matthew 14:19-20).

Through redemption, matter is supernaturally transformed. Well, isn't that what the blood of Jesus has done—supernaturally transformed us? Is not the blood actually supernatural matter? Because of this, all of the physical miracles recorded in the Bible are the result of redemption changing matter.

The same redemption power that changes you from spiritually dead to spiritually living can also enter into matter and change water into wine. When Jesus stopped the storm and walked on water, He had to literally overrule the laws of physics. This is what redemption has the capacity and authority to do—multiply two little loaves of bread and three fishes into enough food to feed more than 5,000 hungry people. Matter had to be changed, created, and multiplied.

Even today, if you have been healed of cancer or a back problem, the redemptive power of Jesus Christ has had dominion over the matter of your physical body. It is by the supernatural blood from His back, or by His stripes, you were healed. Jesus took a physical beating to gain the right as a man to change physical matter.

> *Who Himself bore our sins in His own body on the tree, that we, having died to sins, might live for righteousness—by whose stripes you were healed* (1 Peter 2:24).

So, redemption forgives sins and changes matter. And we know that time, space, and matter are one in perfect continuum so redemption also changes time and space. It is real when Jesus says, "All authority has been given to Me in heaven and on earth" (Matt. 28:18). That includes time. What do you need to turn back your clock to redeem today?

## I Declare in Jesus' Name...

- Jesus is the God of time, space, and matter. He not only created it, He redeemed it for my benefit.
- The laws of nature are subject to Jesus. He is the creator and His command changes time, space, and matter.

- Creative miracles belong to me. Jesus has given me authority to speak that which is not into existence.

- I believe in physical healing. Because it is real, so is Jesus' ability to travel into my past and bring healing to my mind and spirit today.

*Day 27*

# The Matter of Beautiful Timing

*He has made everything beautiful in its time. Also He has put eternity in their hearts, except that no one can find out the work that God does from beginning to end* (Ecclesiastes 3:11).

When the King James boys translated the Bible from Greek and Hebrew into English, there were a few things lost in translation. Don't get me wrong. I believe the Bible is the true and holy Word of God and, as such, is untainted by human influence. With that said, there is a richness to these ancient languages that just doesn't compute to a newer language like English.

Ecclesiastes 3:11 is one of the most prophetically poetic verses in the Bible. It is powerful and touching, but guess what? There's more to this verse than meets the eye. Check out the word *beautiful*. The original word used here was *kairos,* which is a Greek word that literally means "perfect timing."

With that in mind, let's look at the amazing book of Acts. While it's called "The Acts of the Apostles," I see it as the "Acts of the Holy Spirit." Check this out:

> *Now Peter and John went up together to the temple at the hour of prayer, the ninth hour. And a certain man lame from his mother's womb was carried, whom they laid daily at the gate of the temple which is called Beautiful* [perfect timing], *to ask alms from those who entered the temple; who, seeing Peter and John about to go into the temple, asked for alms. And fixing his eyes on him, with John, Peter said, "Look at us." So he gave them his attention, expecting to receive something from them. Then Peter said, "Silver and gold I do not have, but what I do have I give you: In the name of Jesus Christ of Nazareth, rise up and walk." And he took him by the right hand and lifted him up, and immediately his feet and ankle bones received strength. So he, leaping up, stood and walked and entered the temple with them—walking, leaping, and praising God. And all the people saw him walking and praising God. Then they knew that it was he who sat begging alms at the Beautiful Gate* [perfect timing] *of the temple; and they were filled with wonder and amazement at what had happened to him* (Acts 3:1-10).

The family of this crippled man sat him at the "Perfect Timing" Gate every day of his life to beg. Every. Single. Day. Do you know that every person in Israel who ever went to offer sacrifices at the Temple had to walk past that man? Every. Single. One. Year after year, there he was—until he wasn't.

You know it was national news the day that beggar was healed—and he wasn't healed by Jesus. No, sir! His physical healing—the redemption of matter—came from the Holy Spirit through Peter and John—two ordinary men who were demonstrating the Spirit of Power to the world. Jesus walked past that man dozens and dozens of times and never healed him because it was not *kairos*.

You have a *kairos* too and only you know what it is—financial freedom, healing, restoration of family, a ministry, or purpose. Just like that crippled man who got up and danced for joy, your *kairos* moment will be a testimony to the nations of the power of the Holy Spirit. Now, that's beautiful!

## I Declare in Jesus' Name...

- The blood of Jesus and its redemptive power are beautiful. It changes time, space, and matter.
- The Holy Spirit has dominion of my life. He has permission to heal any event, place, or thing in my life that is under a curse.

- The curse of death is reversed over my body, my finances, my family, ministry, purpose, and destiny. Jesus has paid for my full redemption.

- The spirit of infirmity is broken off my body. Jesus died for my healing. His blood is already bringing redemption to my body and mind.

- I am not a beggar but a child of the Most High God. My redemption draws near!

*Day 28*

# Logistical Miracles

*Now when they came up out of the water, the Spirit of the Lord caught Philip away, so that the eunuch saw him no more; and he went on his way rejoicing. But Philip was found at Azotus* (Acts 8:39-40).

Do you see it? There's a flat-out miracle here and it's all about logistics. Philip was obedient to the angel's instructions that he head south on the road to Gaza. What he found there was a very important man—an Ethiopian Jew who happened to be in charge of all Queen Candace's money. He's reading the scroll of Isaiah and scratching his head until Philip shows up.

Philip teaches the man. He gets himself saved and baptized and *boom!* Philip is literally beamed up into space and time. He immediately shows up over 30 miles away in Azotus, which is present day Ashdod. Why? So he could keep preaching and testifying to Jesus to those who had not heard.

"Pastor Troy, I know what the Bible says, but do you really believe Philip time traveled over 2,000 years ago?" Yes, my friend. I do believe that because Jesus can change space and distance because it is in continuum with time.

God picked Phillip up and moved him to another city in the blink of an eye and Philip didn't bat an eyelash. He was not surprised at all! You shouldn't be either. God is not subject to time, space, or matter. He can move and manipulate it any way He wants, and He wanted John to see the future you and I are living in right now.

> *After these things I looked, and behold, a door standing open in heaven. And the first voice which I heard was like a trumpet speaking with me, saying, "Come up here, and I will show you things which must take place after this." Immediately I was in the Spirit; and behold, a throne set in heaven, and One sat on the throne* (Revelation 4:1-2).

God suspended the natural laws to take John on a supernatural trip through time and space. He not only stood in front of God's throne in heaven, that brother was transported across the continents to see things in all corners of the earth, then dropped right back onto the Island of Patmos. He wasn't gone for days or weeks. He was likely gone no more than a few moments or minutes.

The apostle Paul experienced the same thing, and he said he didn't know if his body even went with him!

*And I know such a man—whether in the body or out of the body I do not know, God knows—how he was caught up into Paradise and heard inexpressible words, which it is not lawful for a man to utter* (2 Corinthians 12:3-4).

Can the Lord perform logistical miracles for you? He has for my daughter—three times! On three different occasions, she was driving and immediately found herself miles down the road, parked at her exit, wondering how she got there. One time, she found out there was a massive pileup that she was not a part of. Who knows? Maybe a reckless car was headed her way and God said, "Not today!"

The bottom line is this: Jesus can step into any single timeframe and change it the same as He can heal a human body, reroute a hurricane, unseat a demonic king, or pluck you off I-20 and put you on southbound Highway 67. He's the God of logistical miracles and He's likely got one for you!

## I Declare in Jesus' name...

- Nothing is too hard for the Lord. He can manipulate time, space, and matter for my good any time for all time.
- I trust Jesus with the times of my life. He knows what is best.

- I believe in logistical miracles. God accelerates time-frames to bring me into alignment for my assignment.
- Accelerated trajectory is mine. I will fulfill my identity, purpose, and destiny for the Kingdom.

*Day 30*

# Accelerated Timeframes

*When evening came, his disciples went down to the lake, where they got into a boat and set off across the lake for Capernaum. By now it was dark, and Jesus had not yet joined them. A strong wind was blowing and the waters grew rough. When they had rowed about three or four miles, they saw Jesus approaching the boat, walking on the water; and they were frightened. But he said to them, "It is I; don't be afraid." Then they were willing to take him into the boat, and immediately the boat reached the shore where they were heading* (John 6:16-21 NIV).

Matthew and Mark also tell the story of Jesus walking on the water, and it's just plain glorious. As great as this historical account is, my favorite view of this logistical miracle is through the lens of brother John. Do you know why? Because it's about more than Jesus taking control over matter and using the Sea of Galilee as a sidewalk. He actually accelerates time. Did you see it?

*And immediately the boat reached the shore where they were heading.*

Immediately. That means *boom!* They were on the other side. Time sped up and the boat with all the disciples in it was transported through space and time to the shore of Gadara.

Did you know that accelerated timeframes is a principle in the Bible despite it being totally against the known laws of nature? It sure is. It's when God can't wait another minute to move you into your promise. It's when He has a "suddenly" moment and breaks the speed limit of time to get you to a place where He can bless you to bless others.

He spoke of accelerated time to the prophet Amos, who was a "feller of sycamore trees"—a.k.a. a lumberjack. Fed up with the Jewish people taking advantage of the poor and helpless, he brought a message of repentance during a season of peace and prosperity. He warned the people that calamity was coming if they refused to repent (they refused) and that the Lord was promising restoration if they did.

*"Behold, the days are coming," says the Lord, "when the plowman shall overtake the reaper, and the treader of grapes him who sows seed"* (Amos 9:13).

This is what I call a "right now" word on restoration. In fact, restoration is so important to God that He bestows the blessing before you truly deserve it. Jesus can do that, you know. Bring a harvest in places you have not broken ground or new wine in places you haven't even planted.

My friend, pray for the blessing of accelerated timeframes and accelerated trajectory. The end is greater than the beginning, so pray that God takes you there. Your purpose and destiny await!

## I Declare in Jesus' Name...

- I will harvest where I did not plant and drink new wine that I did not tread. God is restoring me to be a blessing to others.

- Accelerated timeframes are mine. What should take years will now take months or days.

- My purpose and destiny are being fulfilled right now. I walk in accelerated trajectory for new heights, higher levels, and greater anointings.

- The plowman of my life is overtaking the reaper. The power of "suddenly" belongs to me as I bring restoration to the lost and hurting.

*Day 31*

# Stop the World!

*Then Joshua spoke to the Lord in the day when the Lord delivered up the Amorites before the children of Israel, and he said in the sight of Israel: "Sun, stand still over Gibeon; and Moon, in the Valley of Aijalon." So the sun stood still, and the moon stopped, till the people had revenge upon their enemies. Is this not written in the Book of Jasher? So the sun stood still in the midst of heaven, and did not hasten to go down for about a whole day. And there has been no day like that, before it or after it, that the Lord heeded the voice of a man; for the Lord fought for Israel* (Joshua 10:12-14).

Is the Bible really saying that God stopped the world from spinning on its axis so Joshua and the Jewish people could win a battle? Yes, it does. It also says the "sun stood still in the midst of heaven," which means that orbits also ceased. Whaaat?

"Now, Pastor Troy, you said time is relative to the observer. Are you sure the heavens literally stopped moving? Maybe the army was fighting so well and so unified that it just felt like time stood still."

My friend, I'm saying the Word of God says the heavens actually stopped. Why would God stop time for a battle? Is it because He needed the Israelites to win?

Sure, God wanted the Jews to fulfill His covenant and possess the Promised Land, but let's look at the enemy. The Amorites worshiped the sun and moon. They put their trust in the created instead of the Creator and the One True God was making a point—not just to them, but to the Jews.

The Amorites saw their little "g" gods betray them. They discovered the very "deities" they exalted were under the control of the capital "G" God of the Universe. They found out the hard way who the real boss is. Their god was a fake while the God of Israel was the real deal.

And check this out: This happened about 1400 BC. Around that time, the Greek myth of Apollo's son Phaethon disrupting the course of the sun for a whole day started to circulate. The Greeks, who also worshiped the sun and moon, needed an explanation for a very real event they couldn't explain.

Now, it also makes sense that if the sun didn't set in that part of the world for a whole day, there would be a really long night on the other side of the globe, right? Well, the Maori people of New Zealand tell of their demi-god, Maui, slowing the sun to delay its rising, while the Mexican "Annals of Cuauhtitlan" records an unnaturally long night. Hmmm.

The other "why" of this very real historical account is this: Why would God "heed the voice of a man"? Simple. Relationship.

> *So the Lord spoke to Moses face to face, as a man speaks to his friend. And he would return to the camp, but his servant Joshua the son of Nun, a young man, did not depart from the tabernacle* (Exodus 33:11).

Joshua often went with Moses into the presence of God. He could have left with Moses, but he didn't. He knew that God called Moses "friend," and he wanted in on that blessing. While his purpose and anointing as a warrior was different from Moses' destiny as a deliverer and a statesman, the favor of the Lord was on Joshua because he stayed in that tent.

Do you? Do you run to the tent of meeting and stay there when others have left? Going after the presence of the Lord will earn you benefits most people cannot fathom. Who, knows? Maybe Jesus will stop the sun, moon, and stars just for you. I dare you to ask.

## I Declare in Jesus' Name...

- I believe the Word of the Lord. The Bible is true and the accounts in it are reliable.

- What God has accomplished in the past, He can do again. He can part seas, raise the dead, win any battle, and stop time and space at will.
- I am the friend of God. I love His presence and pursue His time and attention.
- The favor of the Lord is upon me. I will serve Him and do His will on earth by loving God and loving people.
- My enemies will not triumph over me. The Almighty God of the Universe is my King. He is on my battlefield and the tide is turning for my victory.

# Day 32

# Reverse the Curse!

*I will make the shadow cast by the sun go back the ten steps it has gone down on the stairway of Ahaz* (Isaiah 38:8 NIV).

This is a game-changer. The Creator of time and space, Jesus, can change and even reverse time. I'm not talking about the spiritual, though He can and does reverse and redeem time in that realm. I'm talking about the natural—a creative miracle of epic proportions. Check this out:

> *Then Isaiah said, "This is the sign to you from the Lord, that the Lord will do the thing which He has spoken: shall the shadow go forward ten degrees or go backward ten degrees?"*
>
> *And Hezekiah answered, "It is an easy thing for the shadow to go down ten degrees; no, but let the shadow go backward ten degrees."*
>
> *So Isaiah the prophet cried out to the Lord, and He brought the shadow ten degrees backward, by which*

*it had gone down on the sundial of Ahaz* (2 Kings 20:9-11).

Just like God halting time so Joshua and his warriors could defeat the Amorites, this defies the known laws of nature. Jesus, as the lawgiver, can suspend and upend those rules whenever He pleases—and it does please Him to give His people a sign and a wonder.

Signs, miracles, and wonders are some of the most powerful voices of God. They don't whisper. They shout! In fact, the Jews were so stiff-necked and removed from the "on-me-presence" of God, the only way He could reach them was with His *omnipresence*.

> *For Jews request a sign, and Greeks seek after wisdom* (1 Corinthians 1:22).

The Lord loved King Hezekiah and gave him a sign to prove that He would, indeed, manipulate time on his behalf. Sick unto death and with the enemy at the gates, Hezekiah was told to get his affairs in order. He was headed to the bosom of Abraham. The king of Judah pulled out the relationship card. Knowing the promised Messiah was to come from his line and having no son, the king made a request of the King of Kings, and God sent him a sign. At Hezekiah's request, the shadow on the sundial of Ahaz moved backward.

Did the sun move? Did the earth reverse its rotation? We don't know and I suppose it doesn't matter. What we do know is Hezekiah's prayer served to reverse the curse of an untimely death and send the enemies of Jerusalem packing. It also fulfilled God's promise that the line of the Messiah would go through Hezekiah as a descendant of David. Hezekiah's son Manasseh was born after this miraculous sign and healing.

Like King Hezekiah, do you need to reverse the curse in your life? Redeem your timeline. Ask Jesus to turn back the shadow and give you a sign that His healing blood has turned a great wrong into an eternal right.

## I Declare in Jesus' Name...

- The blood of Jesus has dominion over the hurts, hang-ups, and habits that have been holding me hostage to my history. Lord, reverse the curse my words and actions have brought upon my life.
- The curses in my bloodline are being exposed. Bring them to my mind, Lord, so I can bring them to the Cross for Your redemption.
- The enemy at the gate is defeated. The promises of God for my future are being fulfilled.
- I come out of agreement with the curses in my family line, both spoken and action. These iniquities are cut off right now and will not be plagues to future generations. We are free in Jesus' name!

NOTE: This account of the sundial of Ahaz is the first instance in scripture where any kind of clock or tool for measuring time is mentioned in Jewish culture. Until the days of Daniel over a century later, there was no indication the Jews were breaking the day into hours.

# A Prayer for God to Invade Your Time with Eternity

*Father God, You are welcome in all my times. I pray in the name of King Jesus that Your Kingdom will come into all my days and years—past, present, and future. Where things have been halted, I pray for accelerated timeframes. Let what should take years happen in just a moment so I can get into better places. Lord, let my learning and understanding be as though I have a history, as You did with the first man, Adam.*

*I pray that You would speed up and slow down my experience of time to benefit my relationship with You. Any place in my past where I have missed my calling and purpose, Jesus, visit me in that place and be King of my life. Work all things out for my good. I repent of any time I ran or hid from You and ask that You make Your visible awesomeness manifest in that day and hour. You are my miracle worker.*

*I pray, King Jesus, that You would inhabit my future in glorious places. Invite me there, Lord. Lead and even change my steps in my now to cause me to meet You in my future.*

*Your creation is beautiful, Lord. Establish Your throne in all my house, all my family, all my life, and all my time. In Jesus' name. Amen.*

# Being a King and Priest
## of Your Timeline

Now that you understand time, redemption, and how they work all things (and all times) together for our good, we're going to move to our final premise.

**Premise 5: *We are stewards—not owners—of our lives.***

"Pastor Troy, I get what you're saying, but I don't understand how that fits with redeeming my timeline."

I know it can still be hard to wrap your mind around this revelation in a practical, everyday manner. That's what the following eight lessons are about—biblical points and examples of recognizing places of despair and responding by going after redemption. You can tap into the supernatural act of changing your time to glorify King Jesus. When you glorify Him, it also fixes, heals, and redeems you! When you grasp how to use this in your life today, you, my friend, become a king and a priest over your timeline. Check this out:

> *And* [He] *has made us kings and priests to His God and Father, to Him be glory and dominion forever and ever. Amen* (Revelation 1:6).

A few chapters later, it says,

> *And* [You] *have made us kings and priests to our God; and we shall reign on the earth* (Revelation 5:10).

Being a king is a word on authority in the natural while being a priest is a word on having authority in the supernatural. God wants you to understand this and partner with Him to bring His will for your life to pass.

"But Pastor Troy, won't God bring His will for my life to pass no matter what I do? He is God, after all!"

Both believers and non-believers say, "If it's not of God, it won't work. And if it is God, you can't stop it." While this is true, it's also false and you need to know why.

Let's be clear: There is the will of God that is fixed, permanent, and is going to happen. A good example is Jesus is coming back. Nothing is going to stop Him. You can believe or not—it doesn't matter. Jesus is coming back.

Then there's also the will of God that concerns His heart's desire. That is the plan of God being carried out in your individual life. The problem is, the "in-a-me" often gets in the way and you circumvent God's plan for your good.

I know for a fact that God wanted me to be a preacher who traveled all over the world helping people nobody else would help. Instead of partnering with Him as a kid or a teenager, I had my own dreams and planned a future as a musician. Drugs, alcohol, broken relationships, anger issues, legal troubles—I brought all of these left turns into my life. I was actively derailing God's heart, His will, for my life. I got in the way and so do you, my friend.

How many times have you launched into the next thing—the new job, relationship, financial scheme—only to leave the Lord out of that decision? Finding the will of God demands partnership. Want to find your destiny? Ask God for your identity. Then go after your purpose by asking the Father to reveal His heart for you to you.

> *Ask, and it will be given to you; seek, and you will find; knock, and it will be opened to you* (Matthew 7:7).

That door is to His Heart. Don't take the long way home. Partner with Him on the revelation of redeeming your timeline so His Kingdom can come and His amazing will be done on the earth of your life as He planned it in Heaven. Now, let's you and I get to the business of redeeming your timeline.

## How to Activate Redemption in Your Timeline

1. Ask the Holy Spirit to search your heart and your entire timeline. Give Him full disclosure of your life—the good, the bad, the ugly, the grand—all of it.

2. There will be certain markers where you still experience terrible loss and pain. These are the places where you are going to invite the Lord Jesus Christ to be made manifest in that unredeemed epic event or that season. Write them down.

3. Invite God into that place. Repent and ask Him to have total dominion in that very timeframe. Ask the Lord to show you His presence in that place. Finding Jesus there will change everything for you.

4. Claim and declare your redemption.

5. Commit your life to living from victory in that place because of the blood of the Lamb and the power of redemption.

6. Celebrate your freedom and make a big deal out of your change. Note the changes that happen in your "now" because of the redemption Jesus has brought to that place in time.

7. Live a prophetic and victorious lifestyle dedicated to the contemplation and the celebration of redemption.

# Brace for Impact

*Woe to you, Chorazin! Woe to you, Bethsaida! For if the mighty works which were done in you had been done in Tyre and Sidon, they would have repented long ago, sitting in sackcloth and ashes* (Luke 10:13).

### Point 1: Accountable for the Impact

Maps are very helpful. They set a framework. In fact, looking at a map would make the true meaning of this verse come into sharp focus. Since we have no map, let me draw you one with words.

Chorazin was a Jewish city on a high plateau. Known for its beauty, it overlooked the Sea of Galilee. Bethsaida, too, was located overlooking what is also called Lake Gennesaret and Lake Tiberias. Bethsaida was in the north near the inflow of the Jordan River. Jesus and all His disciples were Jews from this region of Galilee.

In Jesus' time, both Tyre and Sidon were outside the lines. Located on the coast of Lebanon, these two seaport cities were deep in Gentile territory. A quick scan of the Old Testament will show enemy kings and armies, false gods and idols came from Tyre and Sidon. These cities were "out of bounds" for a respectable Jew.

So, what's the big deal? What was Jesus doing in Tyre and Sidon? Signs, miracles, and wonders. He was teaching, healing, and loving on the Gentiles long before the apostle Paul was sent to them. As a matter of fact, He was trying to remain anonymous there, but news got out. The Messiah had come and these Gentiles ran to Him.

This was not the case in Chorazin and Bethsaida. Not only did Jesus start His three-year ministry in the region of Galilee, He and the dirty dozen made numerous pilgrimages to their own hometowns. While they performed miracles, the people there refused to repent—to change. In some cases, people mocked Jesus, dismissing Him as "the carpenter's son," and He was unable to do miracles because of their unbelief (see Mark 6:5; Matt. 13:58).

*For Jesus Himself testified that a prophet has no honor in his own country* (John 4:44).

Those who had been looking for the Messiah missed Him. Those who should have believed did not, even though He was sent for and to them. Jesus was personally offended by this. When He said, "Woe to Bethsaida and Chorazin," He wasn't kidding. Both cities are nothing more than ruins today—missing from the map.

In contrast, Tyre and Sidon are still dots along the coast of Lebanon—thriving cities to this day. They saw, believed, and repented. So what's the moral of this story?

*When Jesus does a miracle, we are held accountable for how that encounter impacts and changes our lives.* That's on us. It is our responsibility. When Jesus begins to move in your life in respect to redeeming your timeline, you are responsible to not only recognize it but let it change you. If you don't, you're off the map, and woe to you!

## I Declare in Jesus' Name...

- I believe Jesus is the God of the miraculous. He wants to do signs and wonders in my life.
- When I call, the Lord answers. I have seen Him work all things for my good.
- I repent of my unbelief. Jesus is not subject to time. He can and will travel through it to bring me the miracle of redemption in my past.
- My future is bright. The redemption Jesus brings has turned mourning to dancing. I am a new creation through the power of redeeming time.

# Healed or Whole?

*And one of them, when he saw that he was healed, turned back, and with a loud voice glorified God, and fell down on his face at his feet, giving him thanks: and he was a Samaritan. And Jesus answering said, Were there not ten cleansed? but where are the nine? There are not found that returned to give glory to God, save this stranger. And he said unto him, Arise, go thy way: thy faith hath made thee whole* (Luke 17:15-19 KJV).

### Point 2: Our wholeness is determined by our thankfulness.

Have you started out to have a "usual" day, but something wonderful happened instead? Well, that's what happened to the lady in this story! In Luke 17, Jesus was on His way to Jerusalem, and the Word says He "passed through Samaria and Galilee." Though the Jews hated Samaritans, and likewise the Samaritans hated Jews, Jesus took His disciples through "enemy territory" many times. On the first occasion, Jesus asked a Samaritan woman of ill repute for a drink of water and revealed Himself as the Messiah she had been looking for. She brought so many non-Jews to Jesus that "the woman at the well" is forever remembered as the first missionary.

On this occasion, word of Jesus' coming has reached the ears of ten lepers—both Jew and Samaritan. Dying by inches, limbs frozen and extremities missing completely, these rotting shells of human flesh dare to hope. They go in search of the Messiah and see Him in the distance entering a village. They cannot follow so they yell at the top of their lungs, "Jesus. Master, have pity on us."

> *So when He saw them, He said to them, "Go, show yourselves to the priests." And so it was that as they went, they were cleansed* (Luke 17:14).

Did Jesus come near? No. We do know the priests, by Jewish law, needed to confirm the leprosy healed. We also know these men were not healed instantly, but as they obeyed and started walking. A miracle for sure, but the best is yet to come!

One of the lepers, a non-Jew, stops in his tracks. Overjoyed and humbled, he turns back. The priest can wait! His grateful heart cannot. He runs to Jesus, shouts praises, falls to the ground in thankful tears at His feet, and gives God glory. In return, Jesus says, "Your faith has made you *whole*."

It's one thing to be healed and have the leprosy gone from your body. It's another to be made whole. Because of his faith and his grateful heart, Jesus restores what this dread disease has taken—ears, fingers, toes, his nose—no longer missing. The man is returned to his pre-leprous state—complete with no scars or marks that he was ever diseased. Jesus redeems his timeline and He can do that for you as well.

*When Jesus does a life-changing miracle for us, our wholeness is determined by our willingness to be truly thankful and appreciative.* Praise, worship, and giving honor to King Jesus qualifies us for the upgrade of wholeness.

When it comes to redeeming time, find Jesus in that place you need redemption. Like the lepers, call out to Him to go into your past. Believe it is done though you don't see or feel any change. I promise you, as you "go on your way," you will suddenly notice a shift. Something will be different. Don't ignore it. Acknowledge it no matter how small and praise Jesus for it. Thank Him and watch how He gives back the days the locusts have eaten (see Joel 2:25) or, in this case, the limbs the leprosy has devoured.

Healed or whole? It's up to you. How much of your timeline will you believe Jesus can redeem? Prove it with praise!

## I Declare in Jesus' Name...

- I am not healed or made whole by what I have done, but because of who Jesus is. He is my Redeemer.

- Redemption is the heart of King Jesus. He is a miracle-working God who loves to make the broken whole.

- I thank Jesus in advance for healing my heart and mind from _____. This curse is now a blessing even though I may not be able to see it.

- All glory be to God for turning back the clock in my life. King Jesus, I thank You for Your blood that heals me and the power of Your Holy Spirit that fills me. I am truly whole because of Your great love.

*Day 35*

# Say, "Yes!"

*And Jesus answered and spoke to them again by parables and said: "The kingdom of heaven is like a certain king who arranged a marriage for his son, and sent out his servants to call those who were invited to the wedding; and they were not willing to come. Again, he sent out other servants, saying, 'Tell those who are invited, "See, I have prepared my dinner; my oxen and fatted cattle are killed, and all things are ready. Come to the wedding."' But they made light of it and went their ways, one to his own farm, another to his business"* (Matthew 22:1-5).

**Point 3: You are responsible to value God's invitation over your agenda.**

An invitation is a big deal. If you don't think so, maybe you've gotten so many of them you don't know the pain and shame of being left out—left on the outside looking in. Maybe you've forgotten those of us who have been passed over time and time again. We are the "uninvited."

We see the wedding photos on Facebook and tell ourselves, "Surely, the venue was small and they just couldn't fit everyone in." We listen to others discuss the next-level birthday bash or family picnic in excited detail while we reason, "I'm sure they meant to call me. They will next time." We suffer the sting and stigma in silence. Let me tell you, friend, if that is you, know that it is me too.

Also know this: The Kingdom of heaven is *not* like that!

In the Kingdom, everyone is invited. Everyone. Every tribe, tongue, sex, age—a very good God has given each of us, including you, a hand-engraved invitation to His wedding feast. His door is open and so is the invitation. All we have to do is say, "Yes."

Remarkably, that invitation in Matthew 22 is not for you to observe a wedding ceremony. It's for you to actually participate as the Bride of Christ! It's the fulfillment of the prophetic picture of the Exodus. The Jews were "called" out of Egypt and brought to the foot of Mt. Sinai. There, God literally asked the nation of Israel to be His bride, and they said, "I do." The Ten Commandments were more than a set of rules to live by, they were a marriage contract to love God and love people.

> *"Now therefore, if you will indeed obey My voice and keep My covenant, then you shall be a special treasure to Me above all people; for all the earth is Mine. And you shall be to Me a kingdom of priests and a holy*

*nation.' These are the words which you shall speak to the children of Israel."*

*So Moses came and called for the elders of the people, and laid before them all these words which the Lord commanded him. Then all the people answered together and said, "All that the Lord has spoken we will do"* (Exodus 19:5-8).

Do you see it? A wilderness wedding. The whole nation recited its vows. Not so today.

While the King is generous and His invitation is open to all, few accept the offer. Why? Read the parable above again. The people "made light of it." That means they didn't think it was any big deal compared to the cares of life. Any excuse will do. "I've got money to make, positions to earn, children to raise, and a trip to the lake planned. I can't today. Maybe tomorrow."

For most, tomorrow turns into next week and next year. Sooner or later, tomorrow never comes. Their invitation has expired and they find the door is shut. Check out the parable of the Ten Virgins. These ten "good girls" were invited to a wedding. Like the people in Matthew 22, half of those with an exclusive invitation made light of it. They didn't even bother to prepare. They missed their own wedding and it cost them everything.

*And at midnight a cry was heard: "Behold, the bride-groom is coming; go out to meet him!" Then all those*

*virgins arose and trimmed their lamps. And the fool-*
*ish said to the wise, "Give us some of your oil, for our*
*lamps are going out." But the wise answered, saying,*
*"No, lest there should not be enough for us and you;*
*but go rather to those who sell, and buy for yourselves."*
*And while they went to buy, the bridegroom came, and*
*those who were ready went in with him to the wedding;*
*and the door was shut.*

*Afterward the other virgins came also, saying,*
*"Lord, Lord, open to us!" But he answered and said,*
*"Assuredly, I say to you, I do not know you"* (Matthew
25:6-12).

My friend, it is one thing for the Lord to invite us into a priv-
ileged and exclusive place as His Bride. *It is totally our responsi-*
*bility to value His invitation more than our own agenda.* It's on
us to show up. That's all we have to do—show up and say, "I'm
so thankful that You have chosen me. I will gladly take my place
at Your table."

When it comes to redeeming your timeline, Jesus has extended
the invitation. Psalm 139:7-9 says He is waiting in your past. He
wants to redeem it so you can reach your full potential, promise, and purpose. The proposal has been made. Have you said,
"I do"?

# I Declare in Jesus' Name...

- God sees me. He loves me and has never forgotten me, even in my darkest hours.
- I say "Yes" to the invitation of God. I gladly take my place at His table.
- I say "I do" to the invitation of Jesus to be His Bride. I will pursue Him into the secret place.
- The cares of life will not keep me from my King! My heart belongs to Jesus and I will not give it to another.

# Dressed for the Occasion?

*But when the king came in to see the guests, he saw a man there who did not have on a wedding garment. So he said to him, "Friend, how did you come in here without a wedding garment?" And he was speechless. Then the king said to the servants, "Bind him hand and foot, take him away, and cast him into outer darkness; there will be weeping and gnashing of teeth"* (Matthew 22:11-13).

**Point 4: The invitation is on God's terms, not yours.**

When Jesus invites you into a redeemed place, you have to be willing to change your garments from sackcloth and ashes to praise—to be willing to live according to a different experience. You are not who you used to be. The old way of living and the "garments" you wore then—hurts, habits, hangups, and homies who, frankly, stink—have gotta go! They don't fit you anymore.

My friend, it is one thing for God to reveal to you His new plan. It's a whole other thing for you to conform your life to the image of that plan. I call that being dressed for the occasion.

You see, *some people accept God's invitation but, like the prideful man in the scripture above, they accept it on their own terms.* They clothe themselves in worldly attitudes, ungodly relationships, and blasphemous beliefs and say, "I'm going to keep my idols and put them right next to God Almighty. He won't mind."

Let me tell you, He does mind. It offends the Lord if we experience His gift of redemption but do not change accordingly. God considers people who do this "lawless," and He has a special place for them.

> *Not everyone who says to Me, "Lord, Lord," shall enter the kingdom of heaven, but he who does the will of My Father in heaven. Many will say to Me in that day, "Lord, Lord, have we not prophesied in Your name, cast out demons in Your name, and done many wonders in Your name?" And then I will declare to them, "I never knew you; depart from Me, you who practice lawlessness!"* (Matthew 7:21-23)

Friend, if you ask Jesus to meet you in your past to redeem a place of defeat, hurt, or shame, recognize the change and live like redemption has come. Remember, it's a gift. When you accept it and wear it with a grateful heart, you'll smell like heaven instead of hell.

## I Declare in Jesus' Name...

- I have accepted the gift of redemption Jesus offers. He is a time traveler and bringing His blood into my past brings healing in my present.

- I am a good steward. I have conformed my life to the image of God's plan. I am dressed for the occasion and accept my place at His table.

- I lay down my pride and my idols of self. I come to You, Jesus, on Your terms, not my own.

- I have taken off the grave clothes of past defeats. Jesus has covered me with love, joy, and peace—and they fit me well! The fragrance of heaven surrounds me.

- My heart is grateful for the gift of free will. I choose this day to follow the Lord and Him only. Old things have passed away and I am made new.

*Day 37*

# Spiritual Beef Jerky

*Therefore know this day, and consider it in your heart, that the Lord Himself is God in heaven above and on the earth beneath; there is no other* (Deuteronomy 4:39).

**Point 5: You are responsible to treasure how God moves in your life.**

A few days ago, we talked about our responsibility to be truly thankful through the outward expression of praise, worship, and telling the whole world what Jesus has done for us through redeeming time. Today, we're going to be a bit more introspective.

When the Lord does an amazing new thing in your life, *it is your responsibility to guard what God has done and keep it special in your life.* You have to value and make a big deal out of this thing called redeeming time by pondering it personally.

*But Mary kept all these things and pondered them in her heart* (Luke 2:19).

That's what Mary did. She pondered. She considered, contemplated, and let the goodness, blessing, and the wonder of it all marinate in her spirit. Throughout her lifetime, I'd guess those treasured moments became revelations of God's love—kind of like the pieces of a puzzle coming together.

When it comes to redeeming your timeline, your ability to hang on to the truth of the Word and the impact of His presence is all about being committed to contemplation. What you meditate or mentally chew on is a skillset developed by recognizing how God moves in your life.

> *I will meditate on Your precepts, and contemplate Your ways* (Psalm 119:15).

When Jesus starts to change your today because He is redeeming your yesterday, hurts and habits will melt away. Your hang-ups? You are no longer imprisoned by them. Everything shifts. Sometimes, He drops a God bomb and you are completely blown away by His love. Want an example?

I asked Jesus to redeem a broken relationship with someone I had wounded deeply growing up. The very day I prayed that prayer, the Lord answered in an explosive way.

His name was Joe. We were in the fifth grade and he had won a big, beautiful blue ribbon during field day at school. I wasn't fast or coordinated, and try as I might, I could not even win a purple ribbon for eighth place. I wanted a ribbon so bad. I wanted to show my family in hopes they would be proud of me.

Waiting for the school bus home, Joe put his ribbon down and went to get a drink. A broken little boy desperate for love and affirmation, I took it. Joe came back and he was devastated. I saw how hurt he was. He cried the whole way home and I saw that pain turn to anger and bitterness as we climbed on that yellow bus.

You see, Joe was poor. And I mean, dirt poor. The kids made fun of him for his worn clothes and shoes. Joe was a good guy, but that didn't matter to the schoolyard bullies. Now, I had become one of them. The ride home was agony for both of us. Even after Joe got off the bus, my guts were churning with guilt and fear. It only got worse when I got home.

The person I had hoped would be proud of me wasn't impressed. They spit chewing tobacco all over that blue ribbon in "approval" of my feat. I couldn't even return it. That wasn't the worst part. Joe's trust was so shattered, he never spoke to any of us boys again. Not. One. Word.

Over the years, I stuffed that whole incident down inside me. There were plenty of failures, betrayals, and broken relationships to pile on top of it. It was all a big, jumbled mess in a dark corner of my past until I was driving to a food outreach 30 years later. For no reason at all, the memory of what I had done to Joe crawled out of the shadows. Talk about a gut punch.

"Lord Jesus," I cried out from that painful place deep inside, "I cannot stand what I did to Joe. I can't stand that it broke him and made him not trust anybody. I can't stand that I took something so special to him—something he earned and deserved—just to please someone who was never going to love me even if I earned every blue ribbon. King Jesus, Sir, I ask You to go back into my timeline, and into Joe's, and apply Your blood to that place. Lord, fix the broken things in him and in me. I don't know how You're going to redeem this, but I know You will because You are good."

I bawled and squalled the whole way to the event. I composed myself and tried to act normal as I was introduced to the crowd. Pastor Troy Brewer was going to give a sermon about service, selflessness, and demonstrating the goodness of God, then pray and lead a team out to feed the hungry. Instead, I crumbled. I found myself in tears. I recounted the very story I just told you to a room full of strangers, telling them how I asked Jesus to travel into the past and fix the mess I had made.

"Troy," said a tall man who had stood to his feet in the middle of the crowd. "Troy, it's Joe. I forgive you." Stunned, I just stood there like a deer in headlights. My brain was calculating the odds and, finding them impossible, I stared at the man and recognized the boy in his face. My heart began to race as Joe said something that slays me to this day: "Troy, I want to know Jesus like you know Jesus. Can you help me do that?" My guilt and shame were blown to smithereens!

I treasure that in my heart. I chew on it like spiritual beef jerky. I contemplate how quickly and completely the Lord brought His blood into my timeline and Joe's. I consider the perfect timing of King Jesus to work all these circumstances together for our good and bring us to a place of full reconciliation and restoration. You can too.

> *Only fear the Lord, and serve Him in truth with all your heart; for consider what great things He has done for you* (1 Samuel 12:24).

## I Declare in Jesus' Name...

- The light of Jesus is exposing my darkness. I will not hide what can be redeemed.
- I will consider the ways of the Lord. He has truly done great things for me.
- I will recognize the fruit of redemption in my life and ponder the love of God in my heart.
- The blood of Jesus is working in my life. I have great expectancy for my future because He has redeemed my past.

*Day 38*

# The Skinny on Redeeming Time

*Then Jacob awoke from his sleep and said, "Surely the Lord is in this place, and I did not know it." And he was afraid and said, "How awesome is this place! This is none other than the house of God, and this is the gate of heaven!" Then Jacob rose early in the morning, and took the stone that he had put at his head, set it up as a pillar, and poured oil on top of it. And he called the name of that place Bethel; but the name of that city had been Luz previously* (Genesis 28:16-19).

### Point 6: You are responsible to let God's goodness impact your life.

You can be in an incredible place and not know it until Jesus shows you. Even though you know it, it is up to you to make that place different from how you once knew it. In the Bible, this is known as renaming a place. Jacob did it after God showed up at a place called Luz, which means "almond tree."

That's not a terrible name for a town, but when God tells Jacob He's going to give the land he's napping on to him and his kids, the wheels start turning in Jacob's head. He wants an upgrade—a "that was then, this is now" place of redemption. When "almond tree" becomes "House of God," Jacob secures a great big blessing for his generations. Boom!

Just like that, there are places in your life you have to give a new, redeemed name because Jesus put His foot down in that place. It has forever changed because how you view it has forever changed.

I know this will surprise you, but I wasn't considered a bright child. As a matter of fact, some said I was too dumb to learn. They sent me to the room with the blue door because they didn't think I would recognize a number. I could draw a car with 50 engines, tell stories and jokes, and create my own comic books. I could sing, play the guitar better than most adults, write songs, and even won a national songwriting competition at age twelve. Still, nobody thought I had promise.

My friend, I grew up surrounded by people who should have loved me, helped me, and believed in me. Instead, they wrote me off. I cannot tell you the impact that had on me. Needless to say, I barely graduated high school.

Enter Jesus Christ. I was a scared, angry 19-year-old kid when I got saved. It was like a bomb going off in my life. Everything changed. The Lord put it in my spirit that, along with my faith package, He had made me a gifted learner. I started getting Holy Spirit downloads on scripture, numbers, stars, dreams, prophecy, and time. He poured into me until the wisdom, insight, and knowledge came rushing right back out of me.

I was such a sponge, I decided to go to Bible college. My papa was so impressed with what the Lord was doing, he emptied his savings to send me to a well-known school of a renowned evangelist and pastor. I was so proud. At last, I would get a degree and accomplish what everyone around me said was impossible.

The campus was beautiful. The kids were from all over the world and they were so nice. Everybody was so nice! I was in paradise—until the second day. During breakfast, the loudspeaker cracked, "Troy Brewer to the administrator's office." I smiled. *They found out I'm a singer-songwriter and they want me to lead worship*, I thought.

Nope. They told me I was too fat to be in Bible college. They told me to look around and, yup, I was the only fat man in sight. As a bad witness to the Lord, I was sent packing. Defeated and humiliated, I called my papa. He came and got me and the six-hour ride of shame began. If that wasn't bad enough, they never gave my papa his money back. It was highway robbery and I was the bleeding man in the ditch.

Fast-forward 25 years. My book *Numbers that Preach* has become so popular it's on the required reading list at seminaries and Bible colleges across the nation. The very institution that said I was too fat to attend now requires its skinny students to read my book. How about them apples?

That is what Jesus does. He goes to places of shame and makes them into places of victory. When you ask Him to redeem those places—those times—He does, and you will see the fruit from that throughout your life. I tell you, I have no ill will against those folks who didn't believe in me. I thank God for them and the testimony of redemption I can be to them today. I'm not even mad at that Bible college. I pray for them to graduate thousands of warriors for the Kingdom.

You see, *it is one thing for God to do a thing, but it is a whole other thing for you to recognize it and let it fully impact and influence your life.* It has mine and it can do the same for you!

## I Declare in Jesus' Name...

- Jesus is exposing the places of pain, failure, and shame in my past. I am putting them on the Lord's altar as sacrifices for redemption.
- I have eyes to see and ears to hear! I am watching with expectancy for the blood of Jesus to redeem my past.
- I embrace what the Lord is doing in my heart, mind, and spirit through redeeming time. Jesus truly is a time traveler working for my good!

- Redemption is pouring out over _____ in my life. What was once a loss is now gain. What was once a place of shame is now a place of victory. My life is transformed!

*Day 39*

# Turn to See the Voice

*And the Angel of the Lord appeared to him in a flame of fire from the midst of a bush. So he looked, and behold, the bush was burning with fire, but the bush was not consumed. Then Moses said, "I will now turn aside and see this great sight, why the bush does not burn." So when the Lord saw that he turned aside to look, God called to him from the midst of the bush and said, "Moses, Moses!" And he said, "Here I am"* (Exodus 3:2-4).

**Point 7: The miracle of redeeming your timeline doesn't change your life until you do.**

God didn't speak to Moses by name until he turned aside to see the burning bush. He had to be willing to investigate further the miracle God was doing.

Once a prince of the most powerful nation on earth, Moses had grown used to disappointment. He didn't fit in with his adopted family. He tried to connect with his true people, the

Jews, but they didn't accept him. To make matters worse, in his desperate attempt to prove he belonged, he killed an Egyptian beating a Jewish slave to death. That got him hated by both camps. With a price on his head and a death sentence waiting for him in Egypt, Moses escaped to the wilderness of Midian at the age of forty.

A desert wasteland, Midian was full of rocks, sheep, and goats. With no other options, Moses became what the Egyptians hated most—a shepherd. They were lower than dirt. Days stretched into years and years into decades. At the age of 80, Moses found somebody he belonged to—God Almighty, the Great I Am.

We all know the account of the burning bush, the Exodus from Egypt, and the parting of the Red Sea, but have you stopped to consider this: How long did Moses stare at the burning bush before he actually "turned to see the voice"? That's right! Just like the apostle John turned to see the voice on the Island of Patmos almost a thousand years later (see Rev. 1:12), Moses responded and it changed everything.

My friend, what if that bush was burning for days or months before he decided to check it out? It's very possible it was burning for years and Moses ignored it. I imagine he said something like, "That's not for me. Miracles don't belong to murderers. Spiritual secrets are not set aside for shepherds. Why get my hopes up only to be disappointed again?" When I think of Moses and the hell he had been through, I tend to believe discouragement was his closest friend—until the Great I Am showed up.

*It is one thing for God to perform a miracle, but it is another thing for you to stop and actually get in front of this miracle.* You have to change your thinking—your belief system about yourself, Jesus, and redemption, before it changes your whole life.

When Moses turned, the voice immediately spoke. When the Lord called him by name, true identity and purpose showed up! Something new had begun to spring up inside him like Jethro's well, only more holy, more satisfying, and very, very real. When Moses set aside the old, God was able to start molding him into the mighty deliverer he was meant to be.

Who are you meant to be? What are you destined to accomplish for the Kingdom? If you go after the revelation and reality of redeeming your timeline, the Lord will be able to call you by name to something you can't imagine. Your past, like Moses', will melt away. Your purpose and destiny will be revealed, and you will witness His wonders!

> *It is the glory of God to conceal a matter, but the glory of kings is to search out a matter* (Proverbs 25:2).

## I Declare in Jesus' Name...

- I have turned to see the voice of the Lord. I am standing on holy ground.

- I give my life—all my life—to the Lord. Jesus, I belong to You and You belong to me.
- I am a friend of God. He accepts me as I am.
- My identity and purpose are rising up inside me. The Holy Spirit is stirring up God's original plan for my life.

*Day 40*

# The Power of Prophetic Acts

*And Elisha said to him, "Take a bow and some arrows." So he took himself a bow and some arrows. Then he said to the king of Israel, "Put your hand on the bow." So he put his hand on it, and Elisha put his hands on the king's hands. And he said, "Open the east window"; and he opened it. Then Elisha said, "Shoot"; and he shot. And he said, "The arrow of the Lord's deliverance and the arrow of deliverance from Syria; for you must strike the Syrians at Aphek till you have destroyed them." Then he said, "Take the arrows"; so he took them. And he said to the king of Israel, "Strike the ground"; so he struck three times, and stopped. And the man of God was angry with him, and said, "You should have struck five or six times; then you would have struck Syria till you had destroyed it! But now you will strike Syria only three times" (2 Kings 13:15-19).*

### Point 8: The level of breakthrough you experience is directly related to your passion.

In both prayer and the prophetic, there is a connection between what God does and what you do. Action and reaction. Just look at Joash, king of Israel. Faced with a formidable enemy, this young ruler asked a dying Elisha to intercede for the nation as the Syrian army was at the gate.

Given a prophetic act of striking arrows against the ground to ensure victory, Joash could have seen his kingdom fully delivered from the enemy, but he was too worried about what others thought. He was skeptical and unbelieving. All he had to do was show some faith in the Lord and strike those arrows on the ground over and over again with conviction, passion, and hope. He didn't, and his nation paid for it.

My friend, God loves a prophetic act, and you tend to walk in power and authority when you understand this. It's this simple: *When God tells you to engage in the power of a prophetic act, your measure of victory is determined by your passionate willingness to respond.*

I know a few things about prophetic acts. I use a replica medieval sword to rebuke tornadoes coming toward my house. I have a prayer pistol named "The Peacemaker" to shoot down the chaos of the enemy with the Prince of Peace. Hebrew prayer shawls, climbing mountains on prophetic dates, and going after the Father's heart at South Padre Island in the middle of winter—well, you get my drift.

The point is, God shows up when I pray, fast, and cry out to Him for 10 days in the desert the first week of January every year. He does! And He shows up when I access His power through the prophetic act of redeeming time. He will for you too!

When you have the faith, conviction, passion, and hope to believe Jesus can and will go into your past to change your present and ensure your future, it moves heaven and earth. So, strike the ground with some arrows. Prophetically turn a clock backward or return to a place of defeat to burn a debt or put a stake in the ground. I promise you, Jesus will show up with redemption and you'll never be the same.

## I Declare in Jesus' Name...

- My confidence is in the Lord. He is the maker and redeemer of time.

- My times are in His hands. I trust the Lord with my past, present, and future.

- I believe Jesus responds to my faith acts. My prayers and prophetic acts will glorify Him.

- Redemption is the currency of heaven. The blood of Jesus is my covering yesterday, today, and forever.

# Prayer for Stewarding and Redeeming Time

Redeeming time is about turning shame, pain, and loss into victory. We've all experienced tragedy and loss. We know the pain and have asked, "Why?" to the heavens only to receive silence in return. The problem is not you or that God isn't listening. The problem is He does not answer the "whys" of life. Why?

Because "why" is wrapped up in accusation. It assumes God is not good. It's also ripe with self-pity and victimhood. "Why" assumes you are good, pure, righteous, and worthy of living a worry-free life full of blessing. What a lie!

There are two questions God will answer without fail when all hell seems to be unleashed on you:

*What does this mean?* (Acts 2:21)

*What do I do with it?* (Acts 22:8)

These are two questions I had to keep in mind when my good friend and record producer, Scotty McKay, died suddenly of a heart attack. He was just finishing what was to be my breakout record when he said he wasn't feeling good. He thought it was heartburn from the Mexican food he'd eaten. Trying to be a smart aleck, I started making fun of him for being old. He was, after all, the Ancient of Days at 51.

I didn't pray for him. I didn't tell him to go to the doctor or offer him a ride. I showed no concern and made a joke. Now he was gone and my record deal was gone with him. Worse yet, Scotty had told me he had a fear of dying alone, and that is exactly what happened. I was overwhelmed with grief, loss, and a horrible feeling of regret.

Was I saved? Yes. Was I forgiven? Yes. However, this place was consuming my peace of mind. It was keeping me from moving forward. It was changing my outlook on life and it needed to be turned from a terrible ending to a victorious beginning.

My friend, this is the first time I asked Jesus to redeem a certain moment in my past. It wasn't pretty, but it was real. I was walking in my cow pasture under the midnight stars. Bawling and squalling, I cried out to heaven, "Lord, I can't stand it that Scotty died alone. He was so afraid."

At that moment, a supernatural clarity hit me as the still, small voice of King Jesus thundered in my spirit, "Ask Me to be with him in those final moments and I will answer your prayer. Trust Me to be there and I will show you I Am."

I instantly knew that though I was subject to the flow of time, Jesus was not. I knew He was a time traveler and going to the past was easy for Him. I began to declare instead of fear. I decreed that God would give Scotty confidence and peace. I rebuked pain and prophesied the comfort of the Holy Spirit. I did this with faith knowing that Jesus had redeemed Scotty's last breaths.

At that moment, everything changed. My experience of this tragic loss changed like a light switching on. Light invaded my darkness. The Lord showed me in my mind Scotty's transition into eternity. It was glorious! Full of laughter and joy. That was in the spiritual.

In the natural, God redeemed my loss and my time by making me a pastor of an awesome church where I can lead worship, sing my songs, and play guitar any time. I write songs, play with world-famous musicians, have shows on both TV and radio, and have rocked out in front of thousands and thousands worldwide. Not bad for a guy who had his music career stolen by the untimely death of a friend.

The bottom line is this: It is never too late to ask the Redeemer into a timeframe of terrible tragedy and change it into a time of great victory.

*Let the redeemed of the Lord say so, whom He has redeemed from the hand of the enemy* (Psalm 107:2).

## How Does This Work?

1. Find a specific moment in time you experienced great loss.

2. Mark the moment. If possible, find the actual date and present your time before the Lord.

3. Confess your feelings or non-Kingdom thoughts you have expressed or harbored. Refuse to be in agreement with them.

4. Literally invite King Jesus into that moment believing it is not too late for Him and that He is willing to do so. Ask Him to appear in that moment of time and in that physical place.

5. Ask the Holy Spirit to supernaturally cause you to perceive His real and tangible presence there. Ask Him to show you, or speak to you, and tell you how He is there, where He is there, and what He is doing.

6. Praise Him for His manifest presence and for how beautiful He is in showing up. Declare His goodness. Proclaim His redemption and righteousness in that place.

7. Ask God to change what flows from that tragedy from a curse to a blessing. Go after advancement, encouragement, and hope as redemption shifts from loss to gain. Death is overcome by life because the presence of King Jesus changes everything.

8.  Ask God to let your "right now" experience change from the tragedy of loss to the blessing of His manifest presence. From that place in time until now, you will continue to be blessed because the Master has redeemed you. Pray for a new time and new flow of time.

9.  Be prepared to acknowledge any new way this becomes manifest or true in your life. Any time you are blessed in that category of your life, recognize it and give God glory.

    *In all your ways acknowledge Him, and He shall direct your paths* (Proverbs 3:6).

10. Grow in the skillset of acknowledging and marking the blessings that come from this redeemed place. How you steward this awareness determines your ability to step into more and more.

    *For I say to you, that to everyone who has will be given; and from him who does not have, even what he has will be taken away from him* (Luke 19:26).

# A Prayer for Redeeming the Time of a Tragic Event

**Mark the day. Name what happened.**

*King Jesus, I lift up the day of _____*
*when _____ happened.*
*This has been a time of great grief and loss for me. I*
*repent for anything I have accused You of concerning*
*this. I am sorry for the problem I have created and the*
*way I have handled it.*

**Call upon His manifest presence in that terrible place.**

*I ask You, King Jesus, to be with me in that very*
*moment. Lord, to cause Your goodness to pass before*
*me in that terrible place and show me Your glory. It is*
*not too late for You to enter into that moment of time.*
*Please be with me, comfort me, and protect me in that*
*place. You have declared You are willing to redeem me*
*and set me free from the terrible thing that happened.*

**Go after the prophetic gift of seeing and personally encountering (tasting) His presence in that place.**

*Holy Spirit, show me the manifest presence of Jesus*
*with me in that place. Show me exactly where He is*

*and what He is doing in that moment. Open my eyes to see Him and open my ears to hear His words in that place.*

**Praise and worship King Jesus in this place.**

*I praise You, my God, that Your goodness overcomes this evil. I praise You for Your heart and for Your power. I declare that God was with me then, is with me now, and will be with me throughout my future.*

**Prophetically declare and celebrate.**

*I declare I have been redeemed and set free from that terrible thief by the blood of the Lamb. Now let my time change! Let the throne of His presence produce life from death and blessings from curses from that very moment into my right-now time. I trust You and have supernatural confidence that You are redeeming my timeline. In Jesus' name. Amen.*

**Be prepared to note and mark the changes that are coming from that redeemed place and time.**

## DESTINY IMAGE BOOKS
## BY TROY BREWER

*Redeeming Your Timeline*

*Redeeming Your Timeline Study Guide*

## About Troy Brewer

Troy Brewer is a tireless student of God's Word and sold-out believer in all things prophetic. Pastor at OpenDoor Church in Burleson, Texas, Troy's radio and television programs are broadcast worldwide. He is a global missionary known for his radical love for Jesus, unique teaching style, and his passion for serving people. Troy rescues girls and boys from sex trafficking worldwide through Troy Brewer Ministries and AnswerInternational.org.

**Keep the revelation of REDEEMING YOUR TIMELINE alive and active in your life with these prophetic resources from Pastor Troy:**

- Redeeming Your Timeline Book
- Redeeming Your Timeline Study Guide
- Supernatural Keys to Redeeming Your Timeline 2-Part Teaching CD/DVD
- Prayers for Redeeming Your Timeline Card
- Prayers for Redeeming Your Timeline Soaking CD
- Redeeming Your Timeline E-Course
- Digital Downloads also available

*Redeeming Your*
# TIMELINE

## BE THE FREEDOM FIGHTER YOU WERE MEANT TO BE!

When you partner with Pastor Troy on a monthly basis to rescue girls and boys from sex slavery worldwide, you'll receive our FREE GIFT of TroyBrewer.TV. Online and available 24-7 from anywhere in the world, this teaching platform includes all Troy's sermons, conferences, podcasts, School of Ministry, School of Prophecy, Revelation Report, Numbers videos and so much more! Partner today.

**You'll be transformed and so will they they!**

**TROYBREWER.COM | 877.413.0888**